❧ A dialogue conteynyng the

number of the effectuall prouerbes in
the Englishe tounge, compact in
a matter concernynge
two maner of ma=
ryages. . .

by
John Heywood.

❦

LONDINI.
ANNO christi.
1562.

A DIALOGUE

CONTAINING THE NUMBER OF THE EFFECTUAL PROVERBS
IN THE ENGLISH TONGUE

PART I. THE PREFACE

Among other things profiting in our tongue—
Those which much may profit both old and
    young,
Such as on their fruit will feed or take hold—
Are our common plain pithy proverbs old.
Some sense of some of which, being bare and
    rude,
Yet to fine and fruitful effect they allude.
And their sentences include so large a reach,
That almost in all things good lessons they
    teach.   [why?
This write I, not to teach, but to touch: for
Men know this as well or better than I.
But this, and this rest, I write for this,
Rememb'ring and considering what the pith
    is :
That, by remembrance of these, proverbs may
    grow.
In this tale, erst talked with a friend, I show
As many of them as we could fitly find
Falling to purpose, that might fall in mind ;
To th'intent that the reader readily may
Find them, and mind them, when he will
    alway.
          Finis.

CHAPTER I.

Of mine acquaintance a certain young man
(Being a resorter to me now and than)
Resorted lately, showing himself to be
Desirous to talk at length alone with me.
And, as we for this a meet place had won,
With this old proverb this young man begun.
Whoso that knew what would be dear,
Should need be a merchant but one year.
Though it, (quoth he), thing impossible be
The full sequel of present things to foresee,
Yet doth this proverb provoke every man
Politically, (as man possible can),
In things to come after to cast eye before,
To cast out, or keep in, things for fore store;
As the provision may seem most profitable,
And the commodity most commendable.
Into this consideration I am wrought
By two things, which fortune to hands hath
     brought.
Two women I know, of which twain the tone
Is a maid of flowering age, a goodly one;
Th'other a widow, who so many years bears,
That all her whiteness lieth in her white hairs.
This maid hath friends rich, but riches hath
     she none,
Nor none can her hands get to live upon.
This widow is very rich, and her friends bare,
And both these, for love, to wed with me fond
     are.   [worse;
And both would I wed, the better and the
The tone for her person, the tother for her
     purse.   [woo.
They woo not my substance, but myself they
Goods have I none and small good can I do.

On this poor maid, her rich friends, I clearly
    know,   [bestow,
(So she wed where they will), great gifts will
But with them all I am so far from faver,
That she shall sure have no groat, if I have
    her.   [swear,
And I shall have as little, all my friends
Except I follow them, to wed elsewhere.
The poor friends of this rich widow bear no
    sway,
But wed her and win wealth, when I will I may.
Now which of these twain is like to be dearest?
In pain or pleasure to stick to me nearest?
The depth of all doubts with you to confither,
The sense of the said proverb sendeth me
    hither,   [scan'd,
The best bargain of both quickly to have
For one of them, think I, to make out of hand.

CHAPTER II.

Friend, (quoth I), welcome! and with right
    good will,
I will, as I can, your will herein fulfil.
And two things I see in you, that show you
    wise.
First, in wedding, ere ye wed to ask advice.
The second, your years being young it appears,
Ye regard yet good proverbs of old ferne years.
And, as ye ground your tale upon one of them,
Furnish we this tale with everychone of them,
Such as may fitly fall in mind to dispose.
Agreed, (quoth he). Then, (quoth I), first this
    disclose—   [maid,
Have you to this old widow, or this young
Any words of assurance ere this time said?

Nay, in good faith! said he.   Well then, (said
      I),
I will be plain with you, and may honestly
And plainly too speak: I like you, (as I said),
In two foretold things; but a third have I
      weighed
Not so much to be liked, as I can deem;
Which is, in your wedding, your haste so
      extreme.
The best or worst thing to man, for this life,
Is good or ill choosing his good or ill wife.
I mean not only of body good or bad,
But of all things meet or unmeet to be had;
Such as at any time by any mean may,
Between man and wife, love increase or decay.
Where this ground in any head gravely
      grateth,
All fiery haste to wed, it soon rebateth.
Some things that provoke young men to wed
      in haste,
Show, after wedding, that *haste maketh waste.*
When *time hath turned white sugar to white
      salt,*   [*malt.*
Then such folk see, *soft fire maketh sweet*
And that deliberation doth men assist,
Before they wed, to *beware of Had I wist.*
And then, their timely wedding doth clear
      appear
That they were *early up, and never the near.*
And once their hasty heat a little controlled,
Then perceive they well, *hot love soon cold.*
And when hasty witless mirth is mated weele,
Good to be merry and wise, they think and
      feel.
Haste in wedding some man thinketh his own
      avail,

When haste proveth *a rod made for his own
      tail.*
And when he is well *beaten with his own rod,
Then seeth he haste and wisdom things far
      odd.*   [need,
And that in all, or most things, wisht at
Most times he seeth, *the more haste the less
      speed.*   [hasty man's foe,
In less things than wedding haste show'th
So that *the hasty man never wanteth woe.*
These sage said saws if ye take so profound,
As ye take that by which ye took your ground,
Then find ye grounded cause by these now here
      told,
In haste to wedding your haste to withhold.
And though they seem wives for you never so
      fit,   [wit
Yet let not harmful haste so far outrun your
But that ye hark to hear all the whole sum
That may please or displease you in time to
      come.   [cheap
Thus, by these lessons, ye may learn good
In wedding and all thing to *look or ye leap.*
Ye have even now well overlooked me, (quoth
      he),
And leapt very nigh me too. For, I agree
That these sage sayings do weightily weigh
Against haste in all thing, but I am at bay
By other parables, of like weighty weight,
Which haste me to wedding, as ye shall hear
      straight.

Nay, in good faith! said he.   Well then, (said
    I),
I will be plain with you, and may honestly
And plainly too speak : I like you, (as I said),
In two foretold things ; but a third have I
    weighed
Not so much to be liked, as I can deem ;
Which is, in your wedding, your haste so
    extreme.
The best or worst thing to man, for this life,
Is good or ill choosing his good or ill wife.
I mean not only of body good or bad,
But of all things meet or unmeet to be had ;
Such as at any time by any mean may,
Between man and wife, love increase or decay.
Where this ground in any head gravely
    grateth,
All fiery haste to wed, it soon rebateth.
Some things that provoke young men to wed
    in haste,
Show, after wedding, that *haste maketh waste.*
When *time hath turned white sugar to white
    salt,*   [*malt.*
Then such folk see, *soft fire maketh sweet*
And that deliberation doth men assist,
Before they wed, to *beware of Had I wist.*
And then, their timely wedding doth clear
    appear
That they were *early up, and never the near.*
And once their hasty heat a little controlled,
Then perceive they well, *hot love soon cold.*
And when hasty witless mirth is mated weele,
Good to be merry and wise, they think and
    feel.
Haste in wedding some man thinketh his own
    avail,

When haste proveth *a rod made for his own
  tail.*
And when he is well *beaten with his own rod,
Then seeth he haste and wisdom things far
  odd.*   [need,
And that in all, or most things, wisht at
Most times he seeth, *the more haste the less
  speed.*   [hasty man's foe,
In less things than wedding haste show'th
So that *the hasty man never wanteth woe.*
These sage said saws if ye take so profound,
As ye take that by which ye took your ground,
Then find ye grounded cause by these now here
  told,
In haste to wedding your haste to withhold.
And though they seem wives for you never so
  fit,   [wit
Yet let not harmful haste so far outrun your
But that ye hark to hear all the whole sum
That may please or displease you in time to
  come.   [cheap
Thus, by these lessons, ye may learn good
In wedding and all thing to *look or ye leap.*
Ye have even now well overlooked me, (quoth
  he),
And leapt very nigh me too. For, I agree
That these sage sayings do weightily weigh
Against haste in all thing, but I am at bay
By other parables, of like weighty weight,
Which haste me to wedding, as ye shall hear
  straight.

His will, for provision to work or neglect.
, But, to show that quick wedding may bring
    good speed,   [deed.
Somewhat to purpose your proverbs prove in-
Howbeit, whether they counterpoise or out-
    weigh
The proverbs which I before them did lay,
The trial thereof we will *lay a water*
Till we try more. For trying of which matter
Declare all commodities ye can devise
That, by those two weddings, to you can rise.

Chapter IV.

I will, (quoth he), in both these cases straight
    show   [grow.
What things, (as I think), to me by them will
And, where my love began, there begin will I
With this maid, the piece peerless in mine eye;
Whom I so favour, and she so favoureth me,
That half a death to us ['tis] asunder to be.
Affection, each to other, doth us so move
That well nigh, without food, we could live by
    love.   [sight,
For, be I right sad, or right sick, from her
Her presence absenteth all maladies quite;
Which seen, and that the great ground in
    marriage
Standeth upon liking the parties personage,
And then of old proverbs, in opening the pack,
One sheweth me openly, *in love is no lack*.
No lack of liking, but lack of living
May lack in love, (quoth I), and breed ill
    chieving.
Well, as to that, (said he), hark this othing :
What time I lack not her, I lack nothing.

But though we have nought, nor nought we
    can geat,
God never sendeth mouth but he sendeth meat;
And *a hard beginning maketh a good ending;*
In space cometh grace, and this further amend-
    ing—
Seldom cometh the better, and *like will to like;*
God sendeth cold after clothes; and this I pike,
She, by lack of substance, seeming but a
    spark,
Steinth yet the stoutest: for *a leg of a lark*
Is better than is the body of a kite;
And *home is homely though it be poor* in sight.
These proverbs for this part show such a
    flourish,
And then this party doth delight so nourish;
That much is my bow bent to shoot at these
    marks,   *[have larks.*
And kill fear: *when the sky falleth we shall* —
All perils that fall may, who feareth they fall
    shall,
Shall so fear all thing, that he shall let fall all;
And be *more fraid than hurt,* if the things were
    doone;   *[moon;*
Fear may force a man *to cast beyond the*
Who hopeth in God's help, his help cannot
    start:
Nothing is impossible to a willing heart.
And will may win my heart, herein to consent,
To take all things as it cometh, and be content.
And here is, (q'he), in marrying of this maid,
For courage and commodity all mine aid.
Well said, (said I), but awhile keep we in
    quench   *[wench.*
All this case, as touching this poor young
And now declare your whole consideration;

What manner things draw your imagination
Toward your wedding of this widow, rich and
    old?
That shall ye, (q'he), out of hand have told.

Chapter V.

This widow, being foul, and of favour ill,
In good behaviour can very good skill;
Pleasantly spoken, and a very good wit;
And, at her table, when we together sit,
I am well served—we fare of the best;
The meat good and wholesome, and whole-
    somely dressed;   [shift—
Sweet and soft lodging, and thereof great
This felt and seen; with all implements of
    thrift,   [coffers;
Of plate and money such cupboards and
And that without pain I may win these proffers.
Then covetise, bearing Venus's bargain back,
Praising this bargain saith, *better leave than
    lack.*
And greediness, to draw desire to her lore,
Saith, that the wise man saith, *store is no sore.*
*Who hath many peas may put the mo in the
    pot;*   [in lot.
Of two ills, choose the least, while choice lieth
Since lack is an ill, as ill as man may have,
To provide for the worst, while the best itself
    save.
Resty wealth willeth me this widow to win,
To *let the world wag,* and *take mine ease in
    mine inn—*   [chin;
He must needs swim, that is hold up by the
He laugheth that winneth. And this thread
    finer to spin,

Maister promotion saieth : make this substance
    sure ;
If riches bring once portly countenance in ure,
Then shalt thou *rule the roost* all round about ;
And better to rule, than be ruled by the rout.
It is said : *be it better, be it worse,*
Do ye after him that beareth the purse.
Thus be I by this once le senior de graunde,
Many that commanded me I shall command.
And also I shall, to revenge former hurts,
Hold their noses to grindstone, and *sit on their*
    skirts
That erst sat on mine. And riches may make
Friends many ways. Thus, *better to give than*
And, to make carnal appetite content,   [*take.*
Reason laboureth will, to win will's consent,
To take lack of beauty but as *an eye fore,*
The fair and the foul by dark are like store ;
When all candles be out all cats be grey ;
All things are then of one colour, as who say.
And this proverb saith, for quenching hot
    desire
Foul water as soon as fair will quench hot fire.
Where gifts be given freely—east, west, north
    or south—
No man ought to look a given horse in the
    mouth.   [*tail—*
And *though her mouth be foul she hath a fair*
I conster this text, as is most my avail.
In want of white teeth and yellow hairs to
    behold,
She flourisheth in white silver and yellow gold.
What though she be toothless, and *bald as a*
    coot?
Her substance is shoot anker. whereat I shoot.
Take a pain for a pleasure all wise men can—

What? *hungry dogs will eat dirty puddings,
man!*
And here I conclude, (quoth he), all that I
know
By this old widow, what good to me may grow.

CHAPTER VI.

Ye have, (quoth I), in these conclusions found
Sundry things, that very savourly sound;
And both these long cases, being well viewed,
In one short question we may well include;
Which is : whether best or worse be to be led
With riches, without love or beauty, to wed;
Or, with beauty without richesse, for love.
This question, (quoth he), inquireth all that I
move.
It doth so, (said I), and is neerly couched,
But th'answer will not so briefly be touched;
And yourself, to length it, taketh direct trade.
For to all reasons that I have yet made,
Ye seem more to seek reasons how to contend,
Than to the counsel of mine to condescend.
And to be plain, as I must with my friend,
I perfectly feel, even *at my finger's end,*
So hard is your hand set on your halfpenny,
That my reasoning your reason setteth nought
But, reason for reason, ye so stiffly lay   [by.
By proverb for proverb, that with you do
weigh,
That reason only shall herein nought move you
To hear more than speak; wherefore, I will
prove you
With reason, assisted by experience,   [hence,
Which myself saw, not long since nor far
In a matter so like this fashioned in frame

That none can be liker—it seemeth even the
    same;
And in the same, as yourself shall espy,
Each sentence suited with a proverb well nigh;
And, at end of the same, ye shall clearly see
How this short question shortly answered may
    be.   *[prick;*
Yea, marry! (quoth he); now *ye shoot nigh the*
Practise in all, above all toucheth the quick.
Proof upon practise, must take hold more sure
Than any reasoning by guess can procure.
If ye *bring practise in place, without fabling,*
I will *banish both haste and busy babling.*
And yet, that promise to perform is mickle,
For in this case my tongue must oft tickle.
Ye know well *it is,* as telleth us this old tale,
Meet that a man be at his own bridal. [were;
If he wive well, (quoth I), meet and good it
Or else as good for him another were there.
But for this your bridal, I mean not in it
That silence shall suspend your speech every
    whit.
But in these marriages, which ye here meve,
Since this tale containeth the counsel I can
    give,
I would see your ears attend with your tongue;
For advice in both these weddings, old and
    young.   [to talk,
In which hearing, time seen when and what
When your tongue tickleth, at will let it walk.
And in these bridals, to the reasons of ours,
Mark mine experience in this case of yours.

Nay, in good faith! said he.   Well then, (said
      I),
I will be plain with you, and may honestly
And plainly too speak : I like you, (as I said),
In two foretold things; but a third have I
      weighed
Not so much to be liked, as I can deem;
Which is, in your wedding, your haste so
      extreme.
The best or worst thing to man, for this life,
Is good or ill choosing his good or ill wife.
I mean not only of body good or bad,
But of all things meet or unmeet to be had;
Such as at any time by any mean may,
Between man and wife, love increase or decay.
Where this ground in any head gravely
      grateth,
All fiery haste to wed, it soon rebateth.
Some things that provoke young men to wed
      in haste,
Show, after wedding, that *haste maketh waste.*
When *time hath turned white sugar to white
      salt,*   [*malt.*
Then such folk see, *soft fire maketh sweet*
And that deliberation doth men assist,
Before they wed, to *beware of Had I wist.*
And then, their timely wedding doth clear
      appear
That they were *early up, and never the near.*
And once their hasty heat a little controlled,
Then perceive they well, *hot love soon cold.*
And when hasty witless mirth is mated weele,
Good to be merry and wise, they think and
      feel.
Haste in wedding some man thinketh his own
      avail,

When haste proveth *a rod made for his own
 tail.*
And when he is well *beaten with his own rod,*
*Then seeth he haste and wisdom things far
 odd.* [need,
And that in all, or most things, wisht at
Most times he seeth, *the more haste the less
 speed.* [hasty man's foe,
In less things than wedding haste show'th
So that *the hasty man never wanteth woe.*
These sage said saws if ye take so profound,
As ye take that by which ye took your ground,
Then find ye grounded cause by these now here
 told,
In haste to wedding your haste to withhold.
And though they seem wives for you never so
 fit, [wit
Yet let not harmful haste so far outrun your
But that ye hark to hear all the whole sum
That may please or displease you in time to
 come. [cheap
Thus, by these lessons, ye may learn good
In wedding and all thing to *look or ye leap.*
Ye have even now well overlooked me, (quoth
 he),
And leapt very nigh me too. For, I agree
That these sage sayings do weightily weigh
Against haste in all thing, but I am at bay
By other parables, of like weighty weight,
Which haste me to wedding, as ye shall hear
 straight.

Hawking upon me, his mind herein to break,
Which I would not see till he began to speak,
Praying me to hear him : and I said, I would ;
Wherewith this that followeth forthwith ·he
     told.

CHAPTER VIII.

I am now driven, (quoth he), for ease of my
     heart
To you, to utter part of mine inward smart.
And the matter concerneth my wife and me,
Whose fathers and mothers long since dead
     be ;
But uncles, with aunts and cousins, have we
Divers, rich on both sides ; so that we did see
If we had wedded, each where each kindred
     would,
Neither of us had lacked either silver or gold.
But never could suit, on either side, obtain
One penny to the one wedding of us twain.
And since our one *marrying, or marring* day,
Where any of them see us, they shrink away,
Solemnly swearing, such as may give ought,
While they and we live, of them we get right
     nought.   [get,
Nor nought have we, nor no way ought can we
Saving by borrowing till we be in debt
So far, that no man any more will us lend ;
Whereby, for lack, we both be at our wits'
     end.
Whereof, no wonder ; since the end of our
     good,
And beginning of our charge, together stood.
But *wit is never good, till it be bought.*
Howbeit, when bought, wits to best price be
     brought ;

Yet *is one good forewit worth two after wits.*
This *payeth me home,* lo! and full mo folly
    hits;
For, had I looked afore, with indifferent eye,
Though haste had made me thirst never so dry,
Yet to drown this drought, this must I needs
    think :
As I would needs brew, so must I needs drink.
The drink of my bride cup I should have for-
    borne,
Till temperance had tempered the taste beforne.
I see now, and shall see while I am alive,
Who weddeth or he be wise shall die · or he
    thrive.
I sing now in this fact, *factus est repente,*
Now mine eyes be open I do repent me :
He that will sell lawn before he can fold it,
He shall repent him before he have sold it.
Some bargains dear bought, good cheap would
    be sold;
No man loveth his fetters, be they made of
    gold;
Were I loose from the lovely links of my chain,
I would not dance in such fair fetters again.
In house to keep household, *when folks will*
    needs wed,   [*bed.*
Mo things belong than four bare legs in a
I reckoned my wedding a sugar-sweet spice;
But *reckoners without their host much reckon*
    twice.   [twain,
And, although it were sweet for a week or
Sweet meat will have sour sauce, I see now
Continual penury, which I must take, [plain.
Telleth me : *better eye out than alway ache.*
Boldly and blindly I ventured on this;
Howbeit, *who so bold as blind Bayard is?*

And, herein, to blame any man, then should I rave
For I did it myself : and *self do, self have.*
But, *a day after fair* cometh this remorse
For relief : for, though *it be a good horse*
That never stumbleth, what praise can that avouch   [touch ?
To jades that break their necks at first trip or
And before this my first foil or breakneck fall,
Subtilly like a sheep, thought I, I shall
Cut my coat after my cloth when I have her.
But *now I can smell, nothing hath no savour* ;
I am taught to know, in more haste than good
How Judicare came into the Creed.   [speed,
My careful wife in one corner weepeth in care,
And I in another; the purse is threadbare.
This corner of our care, (quoth he), I you tell,
To crave therein your comfortable counsel.

CHAPTER IX.

I am sorry, (quoth I), of your poverty ;
And more sorry that I cannot succour ye ;
If ye stir your need mine alms to stir,
Then of truth *ye beg at a wrong man's dur.*
There is nothing more vain, as yourself tell can,
Than to beg a breech of a bare-arsed man.
I come to beg nothing of you, (quoth he),
Save your advice, which may my best way be ;
How to win present salve for this present sore.
I am like th'ill surgeon, (said I), without store
Of good plasters. Howbeit, such as they are,
Ye shall have the best I have. But first declare
Where your and your wife's rich kinfolk do dwell.   [well,
Environed about us, (quoth he), which showeth

The nearer to the church, the farther from God.
Most part of them dwell within a thousand rod;
And yet shall we *catch a hare with a taber*
As soon as catch aught of them, and rather.
Ye play cole-prophet, (quoth I), who taketh in
   hand
To know his answer before he do his errand.
What should I to them, (quoth he), fling or flit?
An unbidden guest knoweth not where to sit.
I am *cast at cart's arse*, some folk in lack
Cannot prease : *a broken sleeve holdeth th'arm
   back;*
And shame holdeth me back, being thus for-
   saken.
Tush, man ! (quoth I), *shame is as it is taken;*
And shame take him that shame thinketh ye
   think none.
Unminded, unmoaned, go *make your moan;*
Till meat fall in your mouth, will ye lie in bed?
Or sit still? nay, *he that gapeth till he be fed*
May fortune to fast and famish for hunger.
Set forward, ye shall never labour younger.
Well, (quoth he), if I shall needs this viage
   make
*With as good will as a bear goeth to the
   stake,*
I will straight weigh anchor, and hoist up sail;
And thitherward hie me *in haste like a snail;*
And home again hitherward *quick as a bee:*
Now, for good luck, *cast an old shoe after me.*
And first to mine uncle, brother to my father,
By suit I will assay to win some favour.
Who brought me up, and till my wedding was
   done
Loved me, not as his nephew, but as his son;
And his heir had I been, had not this chanced,

Of lands and goods which should me much
    avanced.   [bones
Trudge, (quoth I), to him, and on your mary-
Crouch to the ground, and not so oft as once
Speak any one word him to contrary.
I cannot tell that, (quoth he), by Saint Mary !
One ill word axeth another, as folks spake.
Well ! (quoth I), *better is to bow than break—*
It hurteth not the tongue to give fair words ;
The rough net is not the best catcher of birds.
Since ye can nought win, if ye cannot please,
Best is to suffer : *for of sufferance cometh ease.*
Cause causeth, (quoth he), and as cause causeth
    me,
So will I do : and with this away went he.
Yet, whether his wife should go with him or no,
He sent her to me to know ere he would go.
Whereto I said, I thought best he went alone.
And you, (quoth I), to go straight as he is
    gone,
Among your kinsfolk likewise, if they dwell
    nigh.
Yes, (quoth she), all round about, even here
    by.
Namely, an aunt, my mother's sister, who well,
(Since my mother died), brought me up from
    the shell,
And much would have given me, had my
    wedding grown
Upon her fancy, as it grew upon mine own.
And, in likewise, mine uncle, her husband, was
A father to me.   Well, (quoth I), let pass ;
And, if your husband will his assent grant,
Go, he to his uncle, and you to your aunt.
Yes, this assent he granteth before, (quoth
    she),

For he, ere this, thought this the best way
    to be.   [none
But of these two things he would determine
Without aid : for *two heads are better than one.*
With this we departed, she to her husband,
And I to dinner to them on th'other hand.

CHAPTER X.

When dinner was done I came home again
To attend on the return of these twain.
And ere three hours to end were fully tried,
Home came she first : welcome, (quoth I), and
    well hied !
Yea, *a short horse is soon curried,* (quoth she);
But *the weaker hath the worse* we all day see.
After our last parting, my husband and I
Departed, each to place agreed formerly.
Mine uncle and aunt on me did lower and
    glome;   [welcome.
Both bade me God speed, but none bade me
Their folks glomed on me too, by which it
    appeareth :
The young cock croweth, as he the old heareth.
At dinner they were, and made, (for manners'
    sake),
A kinswoman of ours me to table take;
A false flatt'ring filth; and, if that be good,
None better *to bear two faces in one hood.*
She speaketh as she would creep into your
    bosom;   [bottom
And, when the meal-mouth hath won the
Of your stomach, then will the pickthank it tell
To your most enemies, you *to buy and sell.*
To tell tales out of school, that is her great
    lust;

Look what she knoweth, *blab it wist, and out it
    must.*
There is no mo such titifils in England's ground,
To hold with the hare, and run with the hound.
Fire in the tone hand, and water. in the tother,
The makebate beareth between brother and
    brother.
She can wink on the ewe and worry the lamb;
She maketh earnest matters of every flimflam.
She must *have an oar in every man's barge;*
And *no man may chat ought in ought of her
    charge.*
*Coll under canstick, she can play on both
    hands;*
Dissimulation well she understands.
She is *lost with an apple, and won with a nut;*
Her *tongue is no edge tool, but yet it will cut.*
Her cheeks are purple ruddy like a horse plum;
And *the big part of her body is her bum.*
But *little tit-all-tail,* I have heard ere this,
As high as two horse-loaves her person is.
For privy nips or casts overthwart the shins,
He shall lese the mastery that with her begins.
She is, to turn love to hate, or joy to grief,
A pattern *as meet as a rope for a thief.*
Her promise of friendship for any avail,
Is *as sure to hold as an eel by the tail.*
She is *nother fish, nor flesh, nor good red
    herring.*
She is a ringleader there; and I, fearing
She would spit her venom, thought it not evil
To set up a candle before the devil.
I clawed her by the back, in way of a charm
To do me, not the more good, but the less
    harm;
Praying her, in her ear, on my side to hold;

She thereto swearing, by her false faith, she
    would.
Straight after dinner mine aunt had no choice,
But other burst, or *burst out in Pilate's voice:*
Ye huswife, what wind bloweth ye hither this
    night?   [*is light.*
Ye might have knocked ere ye came in; *leave*
Better unborn than untaught, I have heard
    say;
But be ye *better fed than taught,* far away;
Not very fat fed, said this flebergebet;   [jet.
But *need hath no law;* need maketh her hither
She cometh, niece Alice, (quoth she), for that
    is her name,   [shame.
More for need than for kindness, pain of
Howbeit, she cannot lack, for *he findeth that*
    seeks;
Lovers live by love, yea, *as larks live by leeks,* ─
Said this Alice, much more than half in mock-
    age.
Tush! (quoth mine aunt), these lovers in dot-
    age   [courage
Think the ground bear them not, but wed of
They must in all haste; though *a leaf of borage*
Might buy all the substance that they can sell.
Well, aunt, (quoth Alice), *all is well that ends*
    well.   [*end;*
Yea, Alice, *of a good beginning cometh a good*
Not so good to borrow, as be able to lend.
Nay indeed, aunt, (quoth she), it is sure so;
She must needs grant she hath wrought her
    own woe.   [*stone,*
She thought, Alice, she had *seen far in a mill-*
When she gat a husband, and namely such one,
As they by wedding could not only nought win,
But lose both living and love of all their kin.

Good aunt, (quoth I), humbly I beseech ye,
My trespass done to you forgive it me.
I know, and knowledge I have wrought mine
     own pain;
But *things past my hands, I cannot call again.*
True, (quoth Alice), *things done cannot be un-
     done,*
Be they done in due time, too late, or too soon;.
But *better late than never* to repent this.
Too late, (quoth mine aunt), this repentance
     showed is :
When the steed is stolen shut the stable durre.
I took her for a rose, but she breedeth a burr;
She cometh to stick to me now in her lack;
Rather *to rent off my clothes fro my back,*
Than to do me one farthing worth of good.
I see day at this little hole. For *this bood*
Showeth what fruit will follow. In good faith,
     I said,
In way of petition I sue for your aid.
Ah, well ! (quoth she), now I well understand
*The walking staff hath caught warmth in your
     hand.*
A clean-fingered huswife, and an idle, folk say,
And will be lime-fingered, I fear, by my fay !
It is *as tender as a parson's leman—*   [than?
Nought can she do, and what can she have
As sober as she seemeth, few days come about
But she will once *wash her face in an ale clout.*
And then between her and the rest of the rout,
*I proud, and thou proud, who shall bear
     th'ashes out?*   [breathe,
She may not bear a feather, but she must
She maketh so much of her painted sheath.
She thinketh her farthing good silver, I tell
     you;

But, *for a farthing, whoever did sell you
Might boast you to be better sold than bought.*
And yet, though she be worth nought, nor have
    nought,
Her gown is gayer and better than mine.
At her gay gown, (quoth Alice), ye may repine,
· Howbeit, *as we may, we love to go gay all.*
Well, well! (quoth mine aunt), *pride will have
    a fall;*   [*after.*
For pride goeth before, and shame cometh
Sure, (said Alice), in manner of mocking
    laughter,   [*worse*
*There is nothing in this world that agreeth
Than doth a lady's heart and a beggar's purse.*
But pride she showeth none, her look reason
    alloweth,   [*mouth.*
She looketh as butter would not melt in her
Well, *the still sow eats up all the draf,* Alice;
All is not gold that glitters, by told tales.
In youth she was toward and without evil:
But *soon ripe, soon rotten; young saint, old
   devil*—   [*horns.*
Howbeit, Lo God *sendeth the shrewd cow short*
While she was in this house *she sat upon
   thorns,*
Each one day was three till liberty was borrow,
For one month's joy to bring her whole life's
    sorrow.   [*well;*
It were pity, (quoth Alice), but she should do
For beauty and stature *she beareth the bell.*
Ill weed groweth fast, Alice: whereby the corn
   is lorne;
For surely the weed overgroweth the corn.
Ye praise the wine before ye taste of the grape:
But *she can no more harm than can a she ape.*
It is a good body, her property preves

She lacketh but even a new pair of sleeves.
If I may, (as they say), tell truth without sin,
Of truth she is *a wolf in a lamb's skin.*
Her heart is full high when her eye is full low—
A guest as good lost as found, for all this
    show—
But *many a good cow hath an evil calf.*
I speak this, daughter, in thy mother's behalf,
My sister, (God rest her soul!) whom, though I
    boast,
Was called the flower of honesty in this coast.
Aunt, (quoth I), I take for father and mother
Mine uncle and you, above all other.
When we would, ye would not be our child,
    (quoth she),   [we;
Wherefore now when ye would, now will not
Since thou wouldst needs cast away thyself
    thus,
Thou shalt sure sink in thine own sin for us.
Aunt, (quoth I), *after a doting or drunken
    deed,*
Let submission obtain some mercy or meed.
He that killeth a man when he is drunk, (quoth
    she),
Shall be hanged when he is sober; and he,
Whom in itching no scratching will forbear,
*He must bear the smarting that shall follow
    there.*
And thou, being borne very nigh of my stock,
*Though nigh be my kirtle, yet near is my
    smock—*
I have one of mine own whom I must look to.
Yea, aunt, (quoth Alice), that thing must ye
    needs do;
Nature compelleth you to set your own first up;
For I have heard say, *it is a dear collop*

That is cut out of th'own flesh. But yet, aunt,
So small may her request be, that ye may grant
To satisfy the same, which may do her good,
And you no harm in th'avancing your own blood. [crave,
And cousin, (quoth she to me), what ye would
Declare, that our aunt may know what ye would have.
Nay, (quoth I), be they winners or losers,
Folk say alway *beggars should be no choosers.* [please;
With thanks I shall take whatever mine aunt
Where nothing is, a little thing doth ease;
Hunger maketh hard beans sweet; where saddles lack, [back.
Better ride on a pad than on the horse bare
And by this proverb appeareth this o'thing :
That alway *somewhat is better than nothing.*
Hold fast when ye have it, (quoth she), by my life ! [wife,
The boy thy husband, and thou the girl, his
Shall not consume that I have laboured for.
Thou art young enough, and I can work no more.
Kit Callot, my cousin, saw this thus far on,
And in mine aunt's ear she whispereth anon,
Roundly these words, to make this matter whole :
Aunt, *let them that be a-cold blow at the coal.*
They shall for me, Alice, (quoth she), by God's blist !
She and I have shaken hands : farewell, un-kissed !
And thus, with a beck as good as a dieu gard,
She flang fro me, and I from her hitherward.

Begging of her booteth *not the worth of a*
   bean;   [*mean.*
Little knoweth the fat sow what the lean doth
Forsooth! (quoth I), ye have bestirred ye
   well—   [fell?
But where was your uncle while all this fray
Asleep by, (quoth she), routing like a hog;
And *it is evil waking of a sleeping dog.*
The bitch and her whelp might have been
   asleep too,
For ought they in waking to me would do.
Fare ye well! (quoth she); I will now home
   straight,   [wait.
And at my husband's hands for better news

CHAPTER XI.

He came home to me the next day before noon:
What tidings now, (quoth I), how have ye
   doon?
Upon our departing, (quoth he), yesterday,
Toward mine uncle's, somewhat more than
   midway,
I overtook a man, a servant of his,
And a friend of mine; who guessed straight
   with this
What mine errand was, offering in the same
To do his best for me; and so, in God's name
Thither we went; nobody being within
But mine uncle, mine aunt, and one of our
   kin—
A mad knave, as it were a railing jester,
Not a more gaggling gander hence to Chester.
At sight of me he asked, who have we there?
I have seen this gentleman, if I wist where;
Howbeit, lo! *seldom seen, soon forgotten.*

He was, (as he will be), somewhat cupshotten :
Six days in the week, beside the market day,
Malt is above wheat with him, market men say.
But forasmuch as I saw the same taunt
Contented well mine uncle and mine aunt,
And that *I came to fall in and not to fall out,*
I forbear; or else his drunken red snout
I would have made *as oft change from hue
to hue*
As doth the cocks of Ind; for this is true :
It is a small hop on my thumb; and Christ wot,
It is wood at a word—*little pot soon hot.*
Now *merry as a cricket,* and by and by
Angry as a wasp, though in both no cause why.
But he was at home there, he might speak his
will :
Every cock is proud on his own dunghill.
I shall be even with him herein when I can.
But he, having done, thus mine uncle began :
Ye merchant ! what attempteth you to attempt
us,
To come on us before the messenger thus?
Roaming in and out, I hear tell how ye toss;
But son, *the rolling stone never gathereth
moss.*
Like a pickpurse pilgrim ye pry and ye prowl
At rovers, *to rob Peter and pay Poule.*
Iwys, I know, or any more be told,
That *draf is your errand, but drink ye wolde.*
Uncle, (quoth I), of the cause for which I
come
I pray you patiently hear the whole sum.
In faith ! (quoth he), without any more
summing,
I know to beg of me is thy coming.
Forsooth ! (quoth his man), it is so, indeed;

And I dare boldly boast, if ye knew his need,
Ye would of pity yet fet him in some stay.
Son, *better be envied than pitied*, folk say;
And for his cause of pity, (had he had grace), /
He might this day have been *clear out of the
    case;   [frog—*
But now *he hath well fished and caught a
Where nought is to wed with, wise men flee the
    clog.*
Where I, (quoth I), did not as ye willed or bad,
That repent I oft, and as oft wish I had.
Son, (quoth he), as I have heard of mine olders,
*Wishers and woulders be no good house-
    holders:*
This proverb for a lesson, with such other.
Not like, (as who sayeth), the son of my
    brother,
But like mine own son, I oft before told thee
To cast her quite off; but it would not hold thee
When I willed thee any other where to go—
Tush! there was *no mo maids but malkin*
    though
Ye had been lost to lack your lust when ye list,
By two miles trudging twice a week to be
    kissed.
I would ye had kissed—well I will no more stir:
It is good to have a hatch before the dur.
But *who will, in time present, pleasure refrain
Shall, in time to come, the more pleasure
    obtain.*
*Follow pleasure, and then will pleasure flee;
Flee pleasure, and pleasure will follow thee.*
And how is my saying come to pass now?
How oft did I prophesy this between you
And your ginifinee nycebecetur?   [petre?
When sweet sugar should turn to sour salt-

Whereby ye should in saying that ye never
    saw,
Think that you never thought yourself a daw.
But that time ye thought me a daw, so that I
Did no good in all my words then, save only
Approved this proverb plain and true matter :
A man may well bring a horse to the water,
But he cannot make him drink without he will.
Colts, (quoth his man), *may prove well with*
    tatches ill,
For *of a ragged colt there cometh a good*
    horse—
If he be good now of his ill past no force. [he),
Well, he that hangeth himself a Sunday, (said
Shall hang still uncut down a Monday for me.
I have hanged up my hatchet, God speed him
    well !   [tell :
A wonder thing what things these old things
Cat after kind good mouse hunt; and also
Men say, *kind will creep where it may not go.*
Commonly all thing showeth fro whence it
    came ;
The litter is like to the fire and the dam;
How can the foal amble if the horse and mare
    trot?
These sentences are assigned unto thy lot,
By conditions of thy father and mother,
My sister-in-law, and mine own said brother.
Thou followest their steps *as right as a line.*
For when provender prickt them a little tyne,
They did as thy wife and thou did, both dote
Each one on other; and being not worth a
    groat,   [last,
They went (witless) to wedding; whereby, at
They both went a-begging. And even the like
    cast

HEY. II.   **D**

Hast thou; *thou wilt beg or steal ere thou
  die—*
Take heed, friend, *I have seen as far come as
  nigh.*
If ye seek to *find things ere they be lost,*
Ye shall find one day *you come to your cost.*
This do I but repeat, for this I told thee;
And more I say; but I could not then hold thee;
Nor will not hold thee now; nor such folly feel,
To set at my heart that thou settest at thy heel.
And as of my good ere I one groat give,
I will see how my wife and myself may live.
Thou goest a-gleaning ere the cart have carried;
But ere thou glean ought, since thou wouldst
  be married,   [then?
Shall I make thee laugh now, and myself weep
Nay, good child! *better children weep than old
  men.*   [upon fools;
Men should not prease much to spend much
Fish is cast away that is cast in dry pools.
To flee charge, and find ease, ye would now
  here host—
It is easy *to cry ble* at other men's cost.
But, *a bow long bent, at length must wear
  weak:*   [break.
Long bent I toward you, but *that bent I will*
Farewell, and feed full, that love ye well to do;
But you lust not to do that longeth thereto.
*The cat would eat fish and would not wet her
  feet;*   [in heat.
They must hunger in frost that will not work
And *he that will thrive must ask leave of his
  wife;*   [life,
But your wife will give none: by your and her
It is hard to wive and thrive both in a year.
Thus, by thy wiving, thriving doth so appear,

That thou art past thrift before thrift begin.
But lo! *will will have will,* though will woe
 win;
Will is a good son, and will is a shrewd boy;
And wilful shrewd will hath wrought thee this
 toy.
A gentle white spur, and at need á sure spear;
He standeth now as he had *a flea in his ear.*
Howbeit, for any great courtesy he doth make,
It seemeth the gentle man *hath eaten a steak.*
He beareth a dagger in his sleeve, trust me,
To kill all that he meeteth prouder than he.
He will perk: I here say he *must have the*
 bench—   *[French.*
Jack would be a gentleman if he could speak
He thinketh his feet be where his head shall
 never come;
He would fain flee, but he wanteth feathers,
 some.
Sir, (quoth his man), he will no fault defend,
But *hard is for any man all faults to mend—*
He is lifeless, that is faultless, old folks
 thought.   *[nought.*
He hath, (quoth he), *but one fault, he is*
Well, (quoth his man), *the best cart may over-*
 throw.   [though.
Carts well driven, (quoth he), *go long upright,*
But, for my reward, let him be no longer tarrier,
I will send it him by John Long the carrier.
O! help him, sir, (said he), since ye easily may.
Shameful craving, (quoth he), *must have*
 shameful nay.   *[one yea.*
Ye may, sir, (quoth he), *mend three nays with*
Two false knaves need no broker, men say,
 (said he).
Some say also, *it is merry when knaves meet;*

But *the mo knaves, the worse company to*
　　greet;　　　　　　　　　　　　　[*craveth.*
The *one knave now croucheth while th'other*
But to show what shall be his relevavith,
Either after my death, if my will be kept,
Or during my life : had I this hall hept　[*eat*
With gold, *he may his part on Good Friday*
And fast never the worse, for ought he shall
　　geat.　　　　　　　　　　　　　　[*son :*
These former lessons conned, take for this,
Tell thy cards, and then tell me what thou hast
　　won.
Now, here is the door, and there is the way;
And so, (quoth he), *farewell, gentle Geoffrey!*
Thus parted I from him, being much dismayed,
Which his man saw, and (to comfort me) said :
What, man, pluck up your heart, be of good
　　cheer !
After clouds black, we shall have weather clear.
What, should your face thus again the wool
　　be shorn
For one fall? What, man, *all this wind shakes*
　　no corn!
Let this wind overblow; a time I will spy
To take wind and tide with me, and speed
　　thereby.　　　　　　　　　　　　[*small roast*
I thank you, (quoth I), but *great boast and*
Maketh unsavoury mouths, wherever men host.
And this boast very unfavourly serveth;
For *while the grass groweth the horse sterveth;*
Better one bird in hand than ten in the wood.
Rome was not built in one day, (quoth he), and
　　yet stood
Till it was finished, as some say, full fair.
Your heart is in your hose, all in despair;
But, as every man sayeth, *a dog hath a day—*

Should you, a man, despair then any day?
    nay !
Ye have many strings to the bow, for ye know,
Though I, *having the bent of your* uncle's *bow,*
Can no way bring your bolt in the butt to stand ;
Yet have ye other marks to rove at hand.
The keys hang not all by one man's girdle,
    man ;   [can
Though nought will be won here, I say, yet ye
Taste other kinsmen ; of whom ye may geat
Here some, and there some : *many small make*
    a great.   [curses,
For come light winnings with blessings or
Evermore *light gains make heavy purses.*
Children learn to creep ere they can learn to
    go ;
And, little and little, ye must learn even so.
Throw no gift again at the giver's head ;
-For, *better is half a loaf than no bread.*
I may beg my bread, (quoth I), for my kin all
That dwelleth nigh. Well, yet, (quoth he),
    and the worst fall,
Ye may to your kinsman, hence nine or ten
    mile,
Rich without charge, whom ye saw not of long
    while.
That benchwhistler, (quoth I), is a pinchpenny,
As free of gift as a poor man of his eye.
I shall get a fart of a dead man as soon
As a farthing of him ; his dole is soon done.
He is so *high in th'instep,* and *so straight-*
    laced,
That pride and covetise withdraweth all repast,
Ye know what he hath been, (quoth he), but
    i-wis,
Absence sayeth plainly, *ye know not what he is.*

Men know, (quoth I), I have heard now and
    then,
How the market goeth by the market men.
Further it is said, who that saying weigheth,
It must needs be true that every man sayeth.
Men say also : *children and fools cannot lie—*
And both man and child sayeth, he is a heinsby.
And myself knoweth him, I dare boldly brag,
Even *as well as the beggar knoweth his bag.*
And I knew him not worth a grey groat;
He was at an ebb, though he be now afloat,
Poor as the poorest. And now nought he
    setteth
By poor folk, For *the parish priest forgetteth*
That ever he hath been holy water clerk.
By ought I can now hear, or ever could mark,
Of no man hath he pity or compassion.
Well, (quoth he), every man after his fashion;
He may yet pity you, for ought doth appear,
It happeth in one hour that happeth not in
    seven year.
Forspeak not your fortune, nor hide not your
    need ;
Nought venture, nought have; spare to speak,
    spare to speed;
Unknown, unkissed; it is lost that is unsought.
As good seek nought, (quoth I), *as seek and*
    find nought.
It is, (quoth he), *ill fishing before the net.*
But though we get little, *dear bought and far*
    fet
Are dainties for ladies. Go we both two;
I have for my master thereby to do.
I may break a dish there; and sure I shall
Set all at six and seven, to win some windfall.
And I will *hang the bell about the cat's neck,*

For I will first break and jeopard the first
    check.   [mine,
And for to win this prey, though the cost be
Let us present him with a bottle of wine.
What should we, (quoth I), grease the fat sow
    in th'arse,
We may do much ill, ere we do much wars.
It is, to give him, as much alms or need,
As cast water in Thames, or as good a deed
As it is *to help a dog over a stile.*   [while.
Then go we, (quoth he), we lese time all this
To follow his fancy we went together, [thither,
And toward night yesternight when we came
She was within, but he was yet abroad. [toad,
And straight as she saw me she swelled like a
Pattering the devil's Pater noster to herself :
God never made a more crabbed elf !
She bade him welcome, but the worse for me;
This knave cometh a-begging by me, thought
    she.   [*wind ;*
I smelled her out, and *had her straight in the*
She may abide no beggars of any kind.
They be both greedy guts all given to get
They care not how : *all is fish that cometh to*
    net.   [*ning*
They know no end of their good; nor begin-
Of any goodness : such is wretched winning.
Hunger droppeth even out of both their noses.
She goeth with broken shoon and torn hoses;
But *who is worse shod than the shoemaker's*
    wife,
With shops full of new shoes all her life?
Or *who will do less than they that may do*
    most?
And namely of her I can no way make boast.
She is *one of them to whom God bade ho;*

She will all have, and will right nought forego;
She will not part with the paring of her nails;
She toileth continually for avails;
Which life she hath so long now kept in ure,
That for no life she would make change, be
    sure.
But this lesson learned I, ere I was years seven:
They that be in hell ween there is none other
    heaven.
She is nothing fair, but she is ill favoured;
And no more uncleanly than unsweet favoured;
But hackney men say at mangy hackney's
    hire,   [*squire.*
A scald horse is good enough for a scabbed
He is a knucklebone-yard, very meet
To match a minion nother fair nor sweet.
He winketh with the tone eye and looketh with
    the tother;
I will not trust him though he were my brother.
He hath a poison wit, and all his delight
To give taunts and checks of most spiteful
    spite.
In that house commonly, such is the cast,
A man shall as soon break his neck as his fast;
And yet, now such a gid did her head take,
That more for my mate's than for manner's
    sake,
We had bread and drink, and a cheese very
    great;
But *the greatest crabs be not all the best meat.*
For her crabbed cheese, with all the greatness,
Might well abide the fineness, or sweetness.
Anon he came in; and when he us saw,
To my companion kindly he did draw;
And a well favoured welcome to him he yields,
Bidding me welcome strangely over the fields

With these words: Ah, young man! I know
  your matter;
By my faith! you come to look in my water;
And for my comfort to your consolation,
Ye would buy my purse—give me a purgation!
But I am laxative enough there otherwise.
This, (quoth this young man), contrary doth
  rise;
For *he is purse-sick, and lacketh a physician;*
And hopeth upon you in some condition,
Not by purgation, but by restorative,
To strength his weakness to keep him alive.
I cannot, (quoth he), for though it be my lot
To have speculation, yet I practise not.
I see much, but I say little, and do less
In this kind of physic—and what would ye
  guess:
Shall I consume myself to restore him now?
Nay, *backare! (quoth Mortimer to his sow);*
He can, before this time, no time assign,
In which he hath laid down one penny by mine,
That ever might either make me bite or sup.
And by'r lady, friend! *nought lay down, nought
  take up;*
Ka me, ka thee; one good turn asketh another;
*Nought won by the tone, nought won by the
  tother.*   ⌈miles
To put me to cost, thou camest half a score
Out of thine own nest, to seek me in these out
  isles:
Where thou wilt not step over a straw, I think,
To win me the worth of one draught of drink,
No more than I have won of all thy whole
  stock.
*I have been common Jack to all that whole
  flock;*

When ought was to do I was common
    hackney—
Folk call on the horse that will carry alway—
But evermore *the common horse is worst shod.*
Desert and reward be ofttimes things far odd;
At end *I might put my winning in mine eye,*
And see never the worse, for ought I wan
    them by.   [end,
And now, without them I live here at stave's
Where I need not borrow, nor I will not lend.
It is good to beware by other men's harms;
But thy taking of thine halter in thine arms
Teacheth other to beware of their harms by
    thine :
Thou hast stricken the ball under the line.
I pray you, (quoth I), pity me, a poor man,
With somewhat till I may work as I can.
Toward your working, (quoth he), ye make
    such tastings,
As approve you to be *none of the hastings.*
Ye run to work in haste as nine men held ye;
But whensoever ye to work must yield ye,
If your meet-mate and you meet together,
Then shall we see two men bear a feather;
Recompensing former loitering life loose,
As did *the pure penitent that stale a goose*
And stack down a feather. And, where old
    folk tell
That *evil gotten good never proveth well;*
Ye will truly get, and true getting well keep
Till time ye be *as rich as a new shorn sheep.*
Howbeit, *when thrift and you fell first at a*
    fray,   [away.
You played the man, for ye made thrift run
So help me God ! in my poor opinion,
A man might make a play of this minion,

And fain no ground, but take tales of his own
    friends :
I suck not this out of my own fingers' ends.
And since ye were wed, although I nought gave
    you,   [you !
Yet pray I for you, God and Saint Luke save
And here is all : for what should I further
    wade?
I was neither of court nor of council made;
And it is, as I have learned in listening,
A poor dog that is not worth the whistling.
A day ere I was wed, I bade you, (quoth I).
Scarb'rough warning I had, (quoth he), where-
I kept me thence, to serve thee according. [by
And now, if this night's lodging and boarding
May ease thee, and rid me from any more
    charge,   [large.
Then welcome ! or else get thee straight at
For of further reward, mark how I boast me,
In case as ye shall yield me as ye cost me,
So shall ye cost me as ye yield me likewise;
Which is, a thing of nought rightly to surmise.
Herewithal, his wife, *to make up my mouth,*
Not only her husband's taunting tale avoweth,
But thereto deviseth to cast in my teeth
Checks and choking oysters. And when she
    seeth
Her time to take up, to show my fare at best :
Ye see your fare, (said she), *set your heart at
    rest.*
Fare ye well! (quoth I), *however I fare* now;
And well mote ye fare both when I dine with
    you.
Come, go we hence, friend ! (quoth I to my
    mate)—
And *now will I make a cross on this gate.*

And *I*, (quoth he), *cross thee quite out of my
    book*
*Since thou art cross failed; avail, unhappy
    hook!*
By hook or crook nought could I win there;
    men say :
He that cometh every day, shall have a
    cockney;   [hen.
He that cometh now and then, shall have a fat
But *I gat not so much* in coming seeld when,
As a good hen's feather, or a poor eggshell:
As good play for nought as work for nought,
    folk tell.
Well, well! (quoth he), we be but where we
    were;
Come what come would, I thought ere we came
    there,
That *if the worst fell, we could have but a nay.*
There is no harm done, man, *in all this fray;*
Neither pot broken, nor water spilt.
Farewell, he! (quoth I), I will as soon be hilt
As *wait again for the moonshine in the water.*
But is not this a pretty piked matter?
To disdain me, who muck of the world
    hoardeth not,
As he doeth; *it may rhyme but it accordeth not.*
She *foameth like a boar,* the beast should seem
    bold;
For she is *as fierce as a Lion of Cotsolde.*
She frieth in her own grease, but as for my
    part,
If she be angry, beshrew her angry heart!
Friend, (quoth he), he may show wisdom at
    will,   [still :
That with angry heart can hold his tongue
Let patience grow in your garden alway.

Some loose or odd end will come, man, *some
  one day*
From some friend, either in life or at death.
Death! (quoth I), *take we that time to take
  a breath?*
Then graft we a green graft on a rotten root:
*Who waiteth for dead men shoes shall go long
  barefoot.*
Let pass, (quoth he), and let us be trudging
Where some noppy ale is, and soft sweet
  lodging.
Be it, (quoth I), but I would very fain eat;
At breakfast and dinner I eat little meat,
And *two hungry meals make the third a glutton.*
We went where we had boiled beef and bake
Whereof I fed me *as full as a tun;*   [mutton,
And a-bed were we ere the clock had nine run.
Early we rose, in haste to get away;
And to the hostler this morning, by day,
This fellow called, What ho! fellow, thou
  knave!
I pray thee let me and my fellow have
A hair of the dog that bit us last night—
And *bitten* were we both *to the brain* aright.
We saw each other drunk in the good ale glass,
And so did each one each other, that there was,
Save one; but old men say that are skilled :
*A hard foughten field where no man scapeth
  unkilled.*   [the shot;
The reckoning reckoned, he needs would pay
And needs he must for me, for I had it not.
This done we shook hands, and parted in fine;
He into his way, and I into mine.
But this journey was quite out of my way :
Many kinsfolk and few friends, some folk say;
But I find many kinsfolk, and friend not one.

Folk say—it hath been said many years since
    gone—   [deed,
Prove thy friend ere thou have need; but, in-
A friend is never known till a man have need.
Before I had need, my most present foes [goes:
Seemed my most friends; but thus the world
Every man basteth the fat hog we see;
But the lean shall burn ere he basted be.
As sayeth this sentence, oft and long said
    before:
He that hath plenty of goods shall have more;
He that hath but a little, he shall have less;
He that hath right nought, right nought shall
    possess.   [what obtain,
Thus, having right nought, and would some-
With right nought, (quoth he), I am returned
    again.

CHAPTER XII.

Surely, (quoth I), ye have in this time, thus
    worn,
Made *a long harvest for a little corn!*
Howbeit, comfort yourself with this old text,
That telleth us, *when bale is hekst, boot is*
    next;
Though every man may not sit in the chair,
Yet alway the grace of God is worth a fair.
Take no thought in no case, *God is where he*
    was.
But put case, in poverty all your life pass,
Yet poverty and poor degree, taken well,
Feedeth on this: *he that never climbed, never*
    fell.   [somewhere,
And some case, at some time, showeth prefe
That *riches bringeth oft harm, and ever fear,*

Where poverty passeth without grudge of grief.
What, man! *the beggar may sing before the*
And *who can sing so merry a note*   [*thief;*
As may he that cannot change a groat?
Yea, (quoth he), *beggars may sing before
    thieves,*   [*greeves.*
And weep before true men, lamenting their
Some say, and I feel, *hunger pierceth stone
    wall;*
Meat, nor yet money to buy meat withal,
Have I not so much as may hunger defend
Fro my wife and me.   Well! (quoth I), God
    will send   [see.
Time to provide for time, right well ye shall
God send that provision in time! (said he.)
And thus, seeming well-nigh weary of his life,
The poor wretch went to his like poor wretched
    wife: [their knees;
From wantonness to wretchedness, brought on
Their hearts full heavy, *their heads be full of
    bees.*
And after this a month, or somewhat less,
Their landlord came to their house to take a
    stress
For rent; *to have kept Bayard in the stable*—
But that to win, any power was unable.
For, though *it be ill playing with short daggers,*
Which meaneth, that every wise man staggers,
In earnest or boord to be busy or bold
With his biggers or betters, yet this is told:
*Whereas nothing is, the king must lose his
    right.*   [quight.
And thus, king or keyser, must have set them
But warning to depart thence they needed none;
For, ere the next day, *the birds were flown,
    each one*

To seek service; of which, where the man was
    sped,
The wife could not speed; but, maugre her
    head,   [nigh,
She must seek elsewhere, for either there or
Service for any suit she none could espy.
All folk thought them, not only too lither
To linger both in one house together;
But also, dwelling nigh under their wings,
Under their noses they might convey things—
Such as were neither too heavy nor too hot—
More in a month than they their master got
In a whole year.   Whereto folk further weigh-
    ing,
Receive each of other in their conveying,
Might be worst of all; for this proverb preeves :
Where be no receivers, there be no thieves.
Such hap here hapt, that common dread of such
    gyles
Drove them and keepeth them asunder many
    miles.
Thus, *though love decree departure death to be,*
Yet *poverty parteth fellowship, we see;*
And doth those two true lovers so dissever,
That meet shall they seeld when, or haply never.
And thus by love, without regard of living,
These twain have wrought each other's ill
    chieving;   [friends,
And love hath so lost them the love of their
That I think them lost; and thus this tale ends.

CHAPTER XIII.

Ah, sir! (said my friend), *when men will needs marry,*
I see now, how *wisdom and haste may vary:*
Namely, where they wed for love altogether.
I would for no good, but I had come hither.
Sweet beauty with sour beggary! nay, I am gone
To the wealthy withered widow, by Saint John!
What! yet in all haste, (quoth I)? Yea! (q. he);
For she hath substance enough; and ye see
That lack is the loss of these two young fools.
Know ye not, (quoth I), that, after wise men's schools,
A man should hear all parts ere he judge any?
Why axe ye that (quoth he)? For this, (quoth I):
I told you, when I this began, that I would
Tell you of two couples; and I, having told
But of the tone, ye be straight starting away,
As I of the tother had right nought to say;
Or, as yourself of them right nought would hear. [clear
Nay, not all so, (quoth he), but since I think
There can no way appear so painful a life
Between your young neighbour and his old rich wife,
As this tale in this young poor couple doth show;
And that the most good or least ill ye know
To take at end, I was at beginning bent,
With thanks for this and your more pain to prevent,
Without any more matter now revolved,

HEY. II.   E

I take this matter here clearly resolved;
And that ye herein award me to forsake
Beggarly beauty, and rivalled riches take.
That's just, if the half shall judge the whole,
    (quoth I);   [try.
But yet, hear the whole, the whole wholly to
To it (quoth he) then, I pray you, by and by.
We will dine first, (quoth I), it is noon high.
We may as well, (quoth he), dine when this
    is done;
The longer forenoon, the shorter afternoon—
All cometh to one, and thereby men have
    guessed,
Alway the longer east, the shorter west.
We have had, (quoth I), before ye came, and
    syne,
Weather meet to set paddocks abroad in:
Rain more than enough; and *when all shrews*
    have dined,
Change from foul weather to fair is oft inclined.
And all the shrews in this part, saving one wife
That must dine with us, have dined, pair of
    my life!   [ing
Now, if good change of ill weather be depend-
Upon her diet, what were mine offending
To keep the woman any longer fasting?
If ye, (quoth he), fet all this far casting
For common wealth, as it appeareth a clear
    case,   [place.
Reason would your will should, and shall take

THUS ENDETH THE FIRST PART.

PART II

Chapter I.

Diners cannot be long where dainties want;
Where coin is not common, commons must be
    scant.
In post pace we passed from potage to cheese,
And yet this man cried: Alas, what time we
    lese!
He would not let us pause after our repast;
But apart he plucked me straight, and in all
    haste,   [maid,
As I of this poor young man, and poor young
Or more poor young wife, the foresaid words
    had said,
So prayeth he me now the process may be told,
Between th'other young man, and rich widow
    old.
If ye lack that, (quoth I), away ye must wind,
With your whole errand, and half th'answer
    behind.   [you loth,
Which thing to do, since haste thereto showeth
And to haste your going, the day away goeth;
And that time lost, again we cannot win:
Without more loss of time, this tale I begin.
In this late old widow, and then old new wife,
Age and appetite fell at a strong strife:
Her lust was as young as her limbs were old.

The day of her wedding, like one to be sold,
She set out herself in fine apparel.
She was made like a beer pot, or a barrel;
A crooked hooked nose, beetle browed, blear
    eyed.
Many men wished, for beautifying that bride,
Her waist to be gird in, and for a bon grace,
Some well favoured visor on her ill favoured
But with visorlike visage, such as it was, [face.
She smirked, and she smiled, but so lisped this
    lass,   [alone
That folk might have thought it done only
Of wantonness, had not her teeth been gone.
Upright as a candle standeth in a socket
Stood she that day, so *simper-de-cocket.*
Of ancient fathers she took no cure nor care,
She was to them *as coy as a croker's mare.*
She took th'entertainment of the young men
All in dalliance, *as nice as a nun's hen.*
I suppose that day *her ears might well glow,*
For all the town talked of her, high and low.
One said, a well favoured old woman she is;
The devil she is, said another; and to this,
In came the third, with his five eggs, and said,
Fifty year ago I knew her a trim maid.
Whatever she were then, (said one), she is now
To become a bride, *as meet as a sow*
To bear a saddle.   She is, in this marriage,
As comely as is a cow in a cage.
Gup! with a galled back Gill, come up to
    supper !   [*crupper!*
What? *mine old mare would have a new*
And now *mine old hat must have a new band!*
Well, (quoth one), glad is he that hath her in
A goodly marriage she is, I hear say.   [hand;
She is so, (quoth one), *were the woman away.*

Well, (quoth another), fortune this moveth;
And in this case *every man as he loveth*
Quoth the good man when that he kissed his
cow. - [a vow!
That kiss, (quoth one), doth well here, by God
But *how can she give a kiss, sour or sweet?—*
Her chin and her nose within half an inch
God is no botcher, sir! said another; [*meet.*
He shapeth all parts as each part may fit
other. [scanning;
Well, (quoth one), wisely, let us leave this
God speed them! *be as be may is no banning.*
That shall be, shall be; and with God's grace
they shall
Do well, and that they so may, wish we all.
This wonder, (as wonders last), *lasted nine*
days; [their ways,
Which done, and all guests of this feast gone
Ordinary household this man straight began
Very sumptuously, which he might well do
than. [was set
What he would have, he might have; his wife
In such dotage of him, that fair words did fet
Gromwell-seed plenty; and pleasure to prefer,
She made much of him, and he mocked much
of her.
I was, (as I said), much there, and most of all ,
The first month; in which time such kindness
did fall
Between these two counterfeit turtle birds;
To see his sweet looks, and hear her sweet
words, [ure,
And to think wherefore they both put both in
It would have made a horse break his halter
sure. [taught
All the first fortnight their ticking might have

Any young couple their love ticks to have
    wrought.   [*is green.*
Some laughed, and said : *all thing is gay that*
Some thereto said : *the green new broom*
    sweepeth clean.
But since *all thing is the worse for the wearing,*
Decay of clean sweeping folk had in fearing.
And indeed, ere two months away were crept,
And her biggest bags into his bosom swept,
Where love had appeared in him to her alway
Hot as a toast, it grew *cold as a kay.*
He at meat carving her, and none else before,
Now carved he to all but her, and her no more.
Where her words seemed honey, by his smil-
    ing cheer,   [hear.
Now are they mustard, he frowneth them to
And when she saw sweet sauce began to wax
    sour,
She waxed as sour as he, and as well could
    lower.
So turned they their tippets by way of ex-
    change,   [range
From laughing to lowering, and taunts did so
That in plain terms, plain truth to you to utter,
They two agreed like two cats in a gutter.
Marry, sir ! (quoth he), *by scratching and*
    biting   [citing.
Cats and dogs come together, by folks re-
Together by the ears they come, (quoth I),
    cheerly ;
Howbeit those words are not void here clearly.
For, in one state they twain could not yet
    settle,
But wavering as the wind : *in dock, out nettle.*
Now in, now out ; now here, now there ; now
    sad,

Now merry; now high, now low; now good,
    now bad.
In which unsteady sturdy storms strainable,
To know how they both were irrefrainable,
Mark how *they fell out, and* how *they fell in:*
At end of a supper she did thus begin.

CHAPTER II.

Husband, (quoth she), I would we were in our
    nest;   [*rest.*
When the belly is full, the bones would be at
So soon upon supper, (said he), no question
Sleep maketh ill and unwholesome digestion:
By that diet a great disease once I gat. [that.
And *burnt child fire dreadeth;* I will beware of
What, a post of physic, (said she)? Yea, a
    post;
And *from post to pillar,* wife, I have been tossed
By that surfeit.   And I feel a little fit
Even now, by former attempting of it.
Whereby, except I shall seem to leave my wit
Before it leave me, I must now leave it.
I thank God, (quoth she), I never yet felt pain
To go to bed timely; but rising again,
Too soon in the morning, hath me displeased.
And I, (quoth he), have been more diseased
By early lying down, than by early rising.
But thus differ folk, lo! in exercising:
That *one may not, another may.*
Use maketh maistry; and men many times say
*That one loveth not, another doth; which hath
    sped*
All meats to be eaten, and all maids to be wed.
Haste ye to bed now, and rise ye as ye rate;

While I rise early, and come to bed late.
Long lying warm in bed is wholesome, (quoth
    she);   [(quoth he).
While the leg warmeth, the boot harmeth,
Well, (quoth she), *he that doeth as most men do,*
Shall be least wondered on; and take any two
That be man and wife, in all this whole town,
And most part together they rise and lie down.
When birds shall roost, (quoth he), at eight,
    nine, or ten,   [hen?
Who shall appoint their hour—the cock, or the
The hen, (quoth she); the cock, (quoth he);
    just, (quoth she),   [(quoth he).
As Germans lips. It shall prove more just,
Then prove I, (quoth she), the more fool far
    away;
But *there is no fool to the old fool,* folk say.
Ye are wise enough, (quoth he), if ye keep ye
    warm.
To be kept warm, and for none other harm,
Nor for much more good, I took you to wed.
I took not you, (quoth he), night and day to
    bed.
Her carrain carcase, (said he), is so cold
Because she is aged, and somewhat too old,
That she killeth me : I do but *roast a stone*
In warming her. And shall not I save one,
As she would save another? Yes, by Saint
    John !
Ah, sir ! (quoth she), marry ! this gear is alone.
Who that worst may shall hold the candle; I
    see   [me.
I must warm bed for him should warm it for
This medicine thus ministered is sharp and
    cold;   [told.
But *all thing that is sharp is short,* folk have

This trade is now begun, but if it hold on,
Then *farewell my good days! they will be soon*
    gone.   [break.
Gospel in thy mouth, (quoth he), this strife to
Howbeit, *all is not gospel that thou dost speak.*
But what need we lump out love, at once lash-
    ing   [for dashing?
As we should now shake hands? what! soft
The fair lasteth all the year; we be new knit,
And *so late met that I fear we part not yet,*
Quoth the baker to the pillory. Which thing,
From distemperate fonding, temperance may
    bring;   [strong,
And this reason to aid, and make it more
Old wise folk say : *love me little, love me long.* ✓
I say little, (said she), but I think more;
Thought is free. Ye lean, (quoth he), *to the*
    wrong shore.
Brawling booted not, he was not that night bent
To play the bridegroom : alone to bed she went.
This was their beginning of jar. Howbeit,
For a beginning, this was a feat fit,
And but a fleabiting to that did ensue—
The worst is behind; we come not where it
    grew.
How say you, (said he to me), by my wife?
The devil hath cast a bone, (said I), *to set strife*
Between you; but it were *a folly* for me
To put my hand between the bark and the tree;
Or *to put my finger too far in the fire*
Between you, and lay my credence in the mire.
To meddle little for me it is best;
For *of little meddling cometh great rest.*
Yes, ye may meddle, (quoth he), to make her
    wise,
Without taking harm, in giving your advice.

She knoweth me not yet; but if she wax too
    wild   [*child.*
I shall make her know *an old knave is no*
'Slugging in bed with her is worse than watch-
    ing;   [*ing.*
I promise you *an old sack axeth much patch-*
Well, (quoth I), to-morrow I will to my beads
To pray, that as ye both will, so ache your
    heads;
And in meantime, my aching head to ease,
I will couch a hogshead. Quoth he, when ye
    please.
We parted; and this, within a day or twain,
Was raked up in th'ashes, and covered again.

CHAPTER III.

These two days past, he said to me, when ye
    will   ·   [*have Jill.*
Come chat at home; all is well—*Jack shall*
Who had the worst end of the staff, (quoth I),
    now?   [you?
Shall the master wear a breech, or none? say
I trust the sow will no more so deep root.
But if she do, (quoth he), you must set in foot;
And whom ye see out of the way, or shoot
    wide,
Over-shoot not yourself any side to hide;
But shoot out some words, if she be too hot.
She may say, (quoth I), *a fool's bolt soon shot.*
Ye will me to a thankless office hear;
And a busy officer I may appear;
And, *Jack out of office,* she may bid me walk;
And think me *as wise as Waltham's calf,* to
    talk

Or chat of her charge, having therein nought
  to do.
Howbeit, if I see need, as my part cometh too,
Gladly between you I will do my best.
I bid you to dinner, (quoth he), as no guest,
And bring your poor neighbours on your other
  side.
I did so. And straight as th'old wife us espied,
She bade us welcome, and merrily toward me :
Green rushes for this stranger, straw here,
  (quoth she).
With this, apart she pulled me by the sleeve,
Saying in few words : my mind to you to
  meve,
So it is, that all our great fray, the last night,
Is *forgiven and forgotten* between us quite;
And all frays by this I trust have taken end,
For I fully hope my husband will amend.
Well amended, (thought I), when ye both
  relent,   [ment.
Not to your own, but each to other's mend-
Now, if hope fail, (quoth she), and chance
  bring about
Any such breach, whereby we fall again out,
I pray you tell him he's pars vers, now and
  than,
And wink on me. Also hardly, if ye can
Take me in any trip. Quoth I, I am loth
To meddle commonly. For as this tale go'th,
*Who meddleth in all thing may shoe the
  gosling.*   [bring
Well ! (quoth she), your meddling herein may
The wind calm between us, when it else might
  rage.
I will, with good will, (quoth I), ill winds to
  swage,

Spend some wind at need, though I waste wind
    in vain.
To table we sat where fine fare did remain;
Merry we were *as cup and can could hold;*
Each one with each other homely and bold.
And she for her part, made us cheer heaven
    high—
The first part of dinner *merry as a pie:*
But *a scald head is soon broken;* and so they,
As ye shall straight hear, fell at a new fray.

CHAPTER IV.

Husband, (quoth she), ye study, be merry now;
And even as ye think now, so come to you.
Nay, not so, (quoth he), for my thought to tell
    right,
I think how ye lay groaning wife, all last night.
Husband! *a groaning horse, and a groaning
    wife,*   [life.
Never fail their master, (quoth she), for my
No, wife! *a woman hath nine lives like a cat.*
Well, my lamb! (quoth she), ye may pick out
    of that,
*As soon goeth the young lamskin to the market
As th' old ewe's.* God forbid, wife! ye shall
    first jet.
I will not jet yet, (quoth she), put no doubting:
It is a bad sack that will abide no clouting.
And, as we oft see, *the lothe stake standeth
    long,*
So is it an ill stake, I have heard among,
That cannot stand one year in a hedge.
I drink! (quoth she). Quoth he, *I will not
    pledge.*

What need all this? *a man may love his house*
  well
Though he ride not on the ridge, I have heard
  tell. [*stinketh;*
What? I ween, (quoth she), *proffered service*
But *somewhat it is,* I see, *when the cat*
  winketh, [shun;
And both her eyne out; but further strife to
Let the cat wink, and let the mouse run.
This passed, and he cheered us all, but most
  cheer
On his part, to this fair young wife did appear.
And as he to her cast oft a loving eye,
So cast her husband like eye to his plate by;
Wherewith in a great musing he was brought.
Friend! (quoth the good man), *a penny for*
  your thought. [dish.
For my thought, (quoth he); that is a goodly
But of truth I thought: *better to have than*
  wish. [(quoth he)?
What! a goodly young wife, as you have,
Nay, (quoth he), goodly gilt goblets, as here
  be. [show,
By'r lady, friends! (quoth I), this maketh a
To show you more unnatural than the crow:
The crow thinketh her own birds fairest in the
  wood. [stood),
But, by your words, (except I wrong under-
Each other's birds or jewels, ye do weigh
Above your own. True, (quoth the old wife),
  ye say!
But my neighbour's desire rightly to measure,
Cometh of need, and not of corrupt pleasure;
And my husband's more of pleasure, than of
  need. [best feed;
Old fish and young flesh, (quoth he), *doth men*

And some say, *change of pasture maketh fat
    calves.*
As for that, reason, (quoth she), *runneth to
    halves:*
As well for the cow calf as for the bull.
And though your pasture look barrenly and
    dull,
Yet *look not on the meat, but look on the man;*
And whoso looketh on you, shall shortly skan.
*Ye may write to your friends that ye are in
    health;*
But all thing may be suffered saving wealth.
An old said saw: *itch and ease can no man
    please;*
Plenty is no dainty; ye see not your own ease.
I see, *ye cannot see the wood for trees.* [sees
Your lips hang in your light; but this poor man
Both how blindly *ye stand in your own light;*
And that *you rose on your right side* here right;
And might *have gone further and have faren
    worse.*
I wot well I might, (quoth he), for the purse;
But ye be *a baby of Belsabub's bower.* [*sour;*
Content ye, (quoth she)! *take the sweet with the
Fancy may bolt bran and make ye take it flour.*
It will not be, (quoth he), should I die this
    hour,   [eye.
While this fair flower flourisheth thus in mine
Yes, it might, (quoth she), and hear this reason .
    why:

Snow is white,   } *And every man lets it lie.*
And lieth in the dike.

Pepper is black,   } *And every man doth it*
And hath a good smack.   *buy.*

Milk, (q' he), is white, } *But all men know it*
And lieth not in the dike.   *good meat.*

Ink is all black, } *No man will it drink*
And hath an ill smack. } *nor eat.*
Thy rhyme, (quoth he), is much older than
    mine;
But mine, being *newer, is truer* than thine.
Thou likenest now, for a vain advantage, [age,
White snow to fair youth, black pepper to foul
Which are placed out of place here, by rood!
Black ink is as ill meat, as black pepper is
    good; [is ill—
And white milk as good meat, as white snow
But a milk snow-white, smooth, young skin,
    who change will [face?
For a pepper ink-black, rough, old withered
Though *change be no robbery* for the changed
    case, [wit.
Yet shall that change rob the changer of his
For, who this case searcheth, shall soon see in
    it,
That as well agreeeth thy comparison in these,
As alike *to compare in taste, chalk and cheese;*
Or *alike in colour to deem ink and chalk.*
Walk, drab, walk! Nay, (quoth she), *walk,
    knave, walk!*
Sayeth that term. Howbeit, sir, I say not so;
And best we lay a straw here, and even there,
    ho!
Or else this gear will *breed a pad in the straw;*
If ye haul this way, I will another way draw.
Here is God in th'ambry (quoth I)! Quoth he,
    Nay!
Here is *the devil in th'orologe,* ye may say.
Since this, (quoth I), *rather bringeth bale than
    boot,*
Wrap it in the cloth, and tread it under foot.
Ye harp on the string that giveth no melody;

Your tongues run before your wits, by Saint
      Antony !   [(quoth he);
Mark ye, how she *hitteth me on the thumbs,*
And ye taunt me tit over thumb, (quoth she).
Since *tit for tat,* (quoth I), on even hand is set,
Set the hare's head against the goose giblet.
She is, (quoth he), bent to force you, perforce
To know that *the grey mare is the better horse.*
She choppeth logic, to *put me to my clargy:*
She hath *one point of a good hawk; she is
      hardy.*
But wife, *the first point of hawking is hold fast.*
And hold ye fast, I rede you, lest ye be cast
In your own turn.   Nay, she *will turn the leaf;*
And rather, (quoth I), take as falleth in the
      sheaf   [too bold.
At your hands; and let fall her hold, than be
Nay, I will spit in my hands, and take better
      hold.
He, (quoth she), *that will be angry without
      cause,*
Must be at one, without amends; by sage saws.
*Tread a worm on the tail, and it must turn
      again.*
He taketh pepper in the nose, that I complain
Upon his faults, myself being faultless;
But *that shall not stop my mouth,* ye may well
      guess.   [good;
Well, (quoth I), too much of one thing is not
Leave off this !   Be it ! (quoth he), fall we to
      our food;
But *sufferance is no quittance* in this daiment.
No, (quoth she), nor *misreckoning is no pay-
      ment.*   [friend;
But *even reckoning maketh long friends,* my
For *alway own is own at the reckoning's end.*

This reckoning thus reckoned, and dinner once
    done,
We three from them twain departed very soon.

CHAPTER V.

This old woman, the next day after this night,
Stale home to me, secretly as she might,
To talk with me; in secret counsel, (she said),
Of things which in no wise might be bewrayed.
We twain are one too many, (quoth I), for men
    say :
Three may a-keep counsel, if two be away.
But all that ye speak, unmeet again to tell,
I will say nought but mum, and mum is counsel.
Well then, (quoth she), herein avoiding all
    fears,   [*ears.*
Avoid your children : *small pitchers have wide*
Which done, (she said), I' have a husband, ye
    know,   [show.
Whom I made of nought, as the thing self doth
And for these two causes only, him I took—
First, that for my love, he should lovingly look
In all kind of cause, that love engender might
To love and cherish me by day and by night;
Secondly, the substance, which I to him
    brought,   [nought.
He rather should augment, than bring to
But now my good, shall both be spent, ye shall
    see,
And it in spending sole instrument shall be
Of my destruction, by spending it on such
As shall make him destroy me; I fear this
    much.   [*hoop*;
He maketh havoc, and *setteth cock on the*

He is so lavish, the stock beginneth to droop;
And as for *gain is dead and laid in tomb,*
When he should get aught, each finger is a
       thumb;
Each of his joints against other justles,
As handsomely as a bear picketh muscles.
Flattering knaves and flearing queans being the
       mark,   [*wark.*
Hang on his sleeve : *many hands make light*
He hath his hawks in the mew; but, make ye
       sure,
With empty hands men may no hawks allure.
There is a nest of chickens, which he doth
       brood,   [*hood.*
That will sure make his hair grow through his
They can curryfavel; and make fair weather
While *they cut large thongs of other men's*
       leather.
He maketh his marts with merchants likely
To bring a shilling to sixpence quickly.
If he hold on awhile as he begins,
We shall see him prove a merchant of eel-
       skins—
A merchant without either money or ware.
But all be bug's words, that I speak to spare.
Better spare at brim than at·bottom, say I.
Ever spare and ever bare, (saith he), by and by.
Spend, and God shall send, (sayeth he), saith
       th' old ballet,
What sendeth he, (say I), a staff and a wallet?
Then up goeth his staff, to send me aloof;
He is at three words up in the house roof.
And herein to grow, (quoth she), to conclusion,
I pray your aid, to avoid this confusion;
And for counsel herein, I thought to have gone
To that cunning man, our curate, Sir John.

But this kept me back : I have heard, now and
    then,
The greatest clerks be not the wisest men.
I think, (quoth I), whoever that term began,
Was neither great clerk, nor the greatest wise
    man.
In your running from him to me, ye run
Out of God's blessing into the warm sun.
Where the blind leadeth the blind, both fall in
    the dike ;
And, blind be we both, if we think us his like.
Folk show much folly, when things should be
    sped,
To run to the foot that may go to the head.
Since he best can, and most ought, to do it,
I fear not, but he will, if ye will woo it.
There is one let, (quoth she), mo than I spake
    on :
My husband and he be so great, that *the ton*
Cannot piss but the tother must let a fart.
Choose we him aparty, then farewell my part ;
We shall so part stake, that I shall lese the
    whole.   [*sole.*
Folk say of old : *the shoe will hold with the*
Shall I trust him, then ? nay, *in trust is treason.*
But I trust you, and come to you this season
To hear me, and tell me, what way ye think
    best
To hem in my husband, and set me in rest.
If ye mind, (quoth I), a conquest to make
Over your husband, no man may undertake
To bring you to ease, nor the matter amend
Except ye bring him *to wear a cock's comb* at
    end.
For, take that your husband were, as ye take
    him,

As I take him not, as your tale would make
    him,
Yet were contention like to do nought in this
But keep him nought, and make him worse
    than he is.   [clear,
But, in this complaint for counsel quick and
A few proverbs for principles, let us hear:
Who that may not as they would, will as they
    may;   [obey.
And this to this: *they that are bound must*
Folly it is to spurn against a prick;
To strive against the stream, to winch or kick
Against the hard wall.   By this ye may see,
Being bound to obedience, as ye be,
And also overmatched, *sufferance is your dance.*
He may overmatch me, (quoth she), perchance
In strength of body, but my tongue is a limb
To match and to vex every vein of him.
Tongue breaketh bone, itself having none,
    (quoth I);   [awry.
If the wind stand in that door, it standeth
The peril of prating out of tune by note,
Telleth us that *a good bestill is worth a groat:*
In being your own foe, you spin a fair thread.
Advise ye well, for *here doth all lie and bleed;*
Flee th'attempting of extremities all.
Folk say: *better sit still than rise and fall.*
For little more or less no debate make;
At every dog's bark seem not to awake.
And where the small with the great cannot
    agree,
The weaker goeth to the pot, we all day see.
So that *alway the bigger eateth the bean—*
Ye can nought win, by any wayward mean.
Where the hedge is lowest men may soonest
    over:

Be silent! let not your tongue run at rover;
Since by strife ye may lose, and cannot win,
Suffer! *it is good sleeping in a whole skin.*
If he chide, *keep you bill under wing mute;*
Chatting to chiding is not worth a chut.
We see many times, *might overcometh right—*
Were not you *as good then to say the crow is*
white?
And so, rather let *fair words make fools fain,*
Than be plain without pleats, and plant your
own pain.
For, were ye *as plain as Dunstable highway,*
Yet should ye that way rather break a love day,
Than make one thus; though ye perfectly knew
All that ye conjecture to be proved true.
Yet better dissemble it, and shake it off,
Than to broid him with it in earnest or scoff.
If he play *falsehed in fellowship,* play ye
See me and see me not; the worst part to flee.
Why, think ye me so white-livered, (quoth
she), [ye
That I will be tongue-tied? Nay, I warrant
They that will be afraid of every fart
Must go far to piss. Well, (quoth I), your
part
Is to suffer (I say); for ye shall preeve
Taunts appease not things; they rather
agrieve.
But for ill company, or expense extreme,
I here no man doubt, so far as ye deem;
And there is *no fire without some smoke.* we
see. [she):
Well, well! *make no fire, raise no smoke,* (said
What *cloak for the rain* soever ye bring me,
Myself can tell best where my shoe doth wring
me.

But as ye say : *where fire is smoke will appear.*
And so hath it done; for I did lately hear
How flek and his make use their secret haunt-
   ing,   [*ing.*
By one bird, that *in mine ear was late chaunt-*
One swallow maketh not summer, (said I), men
   say.   [*lay,*
I have, (quoth she), *mo blocks in his way to*
For further increase of suspicion of ills :
Beside his jetting into the town to his gills,
With callets he consumeth himself and my
   goods;
Sometime in the fields, sometime in the woods,
Some hear and see him whom he heareth nor
   seeth not—   [wot;
But *fields have eyes and woods have ears,* ye
And also on my maids he is ever tooting.
Can ye judge a man, (quoth I), by his looking?
What, *a cat may look on a king,* ye know !
My cat's leering look, (quoth she), at first
   show,
Showeth me that my cat goeth a catterwawing;
And specially by his manner of drawing
To Madge, my fair maid; for may he come
   nigh her
He must needs bass her, as he cometh by her.
He loveth well sheep's flesh, that wets his
   bread in the wool—
If he leave it not, *we have a crow to pull.*
He loveth her better at the sole of the foot
Than ever he loved me at the heart root.
It is a foul bird that fileth his own nest;
I would have him live as God's law hath ex-
   pressed,
And leave lewd ticking : he that will none ill do
Must do nothing that belongeth thereto;

To tick and laugh with me he hath lawful leave.
To that I said nought, but laughed in my
    sleeve;
But when she seemed to be fixed in mind,
Rather to seek for that she was loth to find,
Than leave that seeking, by which she might
    find ease,
I fained this fancy, to feel how it would please.
Will ye do well? (quoth I), take pain to watch
    him;
And if ye chance in advoutry to catch him,
Then *have ye him on the hip, or on the hurdle;*
Then *have ye his head fast under your girdle;*
Where your words now do but *rub him on the
    gall,*   [wall.
That *deed without words* shall drive him to the
And *further than the wall he cannot go,*
But must submit himself; and if it hap so
That at end of your watch he guiltless appear,
Then all grudge, grown by jealousy, taketh
    end clear.   [she);
Of all folks I may worst watch him, (said
For of all folks himself most watcheth me;
I shall as soon try him, or take him this way,
As *drive a top over a tiled house:* no, nay!
I may keep corners or hollow trees with th' owl,
*This seven years, day and night to watch a
    bowl,*
Before I shall catch him with undoubted evil.
*He must have a long spoon shall eat with the
And *the devil is no falser than is he.*   [*devil;*
I have heard tell, *it had need to be*   [ear—
A wily mouse that should breed in the cat's
Shall I get within him then? nay, *ware that
    gear!*
It is hard halting before a cripple, ye wot;

A falser water drinker there liveth not.
When he hunteth a doe that he cannot avow,
All dogs bark not at him, I warrant yow.
Namely not I, I say, though as I said,
He sometime, though seldom, by some be be-
       wrayed.   [*loweth:*
Close hunting, (quoth I), *the good hunter al-*
But, be your husband never so still of mouth,
If ye can hunt, and will stand at receipt,
Your   maid   examined,   maketh   him   open
       straight.   [preef,
That were, (quoth she), as of my truth to make
To axe my fellow whether I be a thief.
They cleave together like burrs; that way I
       shall
Pike out no more than out of the stone wall.
Then like ye not to watch him for wife nor
       maid?   [I said;
No! (quoth she).   Nor I, (quoth I), whatever
And I mislike not only your watch in vain,
But also, if ye took him, what could ye gain?
From suspicion to knowledge of ill, forsooth!
Could make ye do but *as the flounder doeth—*
Leap out of the frying pan into the fire;
And *change from ill pain to worse is worth*
       small hire.   [doubt;
Let time try!   *Time trieth truth in every*
And *deem the best till time hath tried the truth*
       out.
And reason sayeth: *make not two sorrows of*
       one;
But ye make ten sorrows where reason maketh
       none.   [wink
For where reason, (as I said), willeth you to
(Although all were proved as ill as ye think),
Contrary to reason ye stamp and ye stare;

Ye fret and ye fume, *as mad as a March hare,*
Without proof to his reproof, present or past,
But by such report as most prove lies at last.
And *here goeth the hare away;* for ye judge all,
And judge the worst in all, ere proof in ought
    fall.   [saws;
But *blind men should judge no colours:* by old
And *folk ofttimes are most blind in their own
    cause—*
The blind eat many flies. Howbeit, the fancy
Of your blindness cometh not of ignorancy.
Ye could tell another herein the best way;
But *it is as folk do, and not as folk say;*
For they say, *saying and doing are two things*
To defend danger that double dealing brings :
As ye can seem wise in words, be wise in deed.
That is, (quoth she), *sooner said than done,* I
    drede;
But methinketh your counsel weigheth in the
    whole
To make me *put my finger in a hole;*
And so, by sufferance, to be so lither
In my house *to lay fire and tow together.*
But if they fire me, some of them shall win
*More tow on their distaves than they can well
    spin;*   [hands full—
And the best of them shall *have both their*
Bolster or pillow for me, be whose wull.
I will not bear the devil's sack, by Saint
    Audry !
For concealing suspicion of their baudry.
I fear false measures, or else I were a child;
For *they that think none ill, are soonest be-
    guiled.*
And thus, though *much water goeth by the mill
That the miller knoweth not of,* yet I will

Cast what may scape; and, as though I did
    find it,
With the clack of my mill to fine meal grind it.
And sure ere I take any rest in effect,
I must banish my maids such as I suspect :
Better it be done than wish it had been done.
As good undone, (quoth I), *as do it too soon.*
Well, (quoth she), till soon, fare ye well ! and
    this
Keep ye as secret as ye think meet is.
Out at doors went she herewith; and hereupon
In at doors came he forthwith, as she was
    gone;
And, without any temperate protestation,
Thus he began, in way of exclamation.

CHAPTER VI.

Oh ! what choice may compare to the devil's
    life
Like his that have chosen a devil to his wife?
Namely, such an old witch, such a macka-
    broine,
As evermore *like a hog hangeth the groyne*
On her husband, except he be her slave,
And follow all fancies that she would have.
'Tis said : *there is no good accord*
Where every man would be a lord.
Wherefore, my wife will be no lord, but lady,
To make me, that should be her lord, a baby.
Before I was wedded, and since, I made
    reckoning
To make my wife bow at every beckoning.
Bachelors boast how they will teach their
    wives good;

But *many a man speaketh of Robin Hood*
That never shot in his bow. When all is
    sought,   [*taught.*
Bachelors' wives, and maids' children be well
And this with this, I also begin to gather:
Every man can rule a shrew, save he that hath
    her.   [like wax;
At my will I weened she should have wrought
But I find and feel she hath found *such knacks*
In her bouget, and *such toys in her head,*
That to dance after her pipe I am nigh led.
It is said of old: *an old dog biteth sore;*
But, by God! th' old bitch biteth sorer and
    more;   [her tongue.
And not with teeth—(she hath none)—but with
If all tales be true, (quoth I), though she be
    stung,   [blame;
And thereby sting you, she is not much to
For, whatever you say, thus goeth the same.
When folk first saw your substance laid in
    your lap,   [good hap,
Without your pain, with your wife brought by
Oft in remembrance of haps happy device
They would say: *better to be happy than wise;*
Not minding thereby then to deprave your wit,
For they had good hope to see good proof of it.
But since their good opinion therein so cools,
That they say as oft: *God sendeth fortune to*
    fools;
In that, as fortune without your wit gave it,
So can your wit not keep it when ye have it.
Sayeth one: *this gear was gotten on a holy*
    day;
Sayeth another: *who may hold that will away.*
This game, from beginning, showeth what end
    is meant:

Soon gotten, soon spent; ill gotten, ill spent.
Ye are called not only too great a spender,
Too frank a giver, and as free a lender;
But also, ye spend, give, and lend, among such
Whose lightness minisheth your honesty as
    much
As your money; and much they disallow
That *ye brike all from her, that brought all to
    yow;*
And spend it out at doors, in spite of her,
Because ye would kill her to be quit of her.
For all kindness, of her part, that may rise,
Ye show all th' unkindness ye can devise.
And where reason and custom, (they say),
    affords
Alway to let the losers have their words,
Ye make her a cuckquean and consume her
    good;
And she must sit *like a bean in a monk's hood.*
Bearing no more rule than a goose turd in
    Thames;
But, at her own maids' becks, wings, or hems,
She must obey those lambs, or else a lambskin
Ye will provide for her, to lap her in.   [say;
This *biteth the mare by the thumb*, as they
For were ye, touching condition, (say they),
The castle of honesty in all things else,
Yet should this one thing, as their whole tale
    tells,
Defile and deface that castle to a cottage—
One crop of a turd marreth a pot of potage.
And some to this cry, Let him pass, for we
    think   [stink.
The more we stir a turd, the worse it will
With many conditions good, one that is ill
Defaceth the flower of all, and doth all spoil.

Now, (quoth I), if you think they truly clatter,
Let your amendment amend the matter:
Half warned, half armed. This warning for
        this I show,   [know.
He that hath an ill name is half hanged, ye

CHAPTER VII.

Well said! (said he). Marry, sir! here is a
        tale—
For honesty, *meet to set the devil on sale.*
But now am I forced *a bead roll to unfold,*
To tell somewhat more to the tale I erst told.
Grow this, as most part doth, I durst hold my
        life,
Of the jealousy of dame Julok, my wife,
Then shall ye wonder, when truth doth define,
How she can, and doth here both bite and
        whine.
Frenzy, heresy, and jealousy are three,
That men say hardly, or never, cured be.
And although jealousy need not or boot not,
What helpeth that counsel, if reason root not?
And in mad jealousy she is so far gone
She thinketh I run over all that I look on.
Take good heed of that, (quoth I), for at a
        word,   [*sword*
The proverb saith: *he that striketh with the*
Shall be stricken with the scabbard. Tush!
        (quoth he),
The devil with my scabbard will not strike me;
But, my dame taking suspicion for full prefe,
Reporteth it for a truth to the most mischief.
In words gold and whole, as men by wit could
        wish,

She will lie as fast as a dog will lick a dish.
She is, of truth, *as false as God is true;*
And, if she chance to see me, at a view,
Kiss any of my maids alone, but in sport,
That taketh she in earnest, *after Bedlam sort.*
The cow is wood; her tongue runneth on pat-
        tens;
If it be morn, we have a pair of matins;
If it be even, evensong, not Latin nor Greek,
But English, and like that as in Easter week.
She beginneth, first with a cry a leison;
To which she ringeth a peal, a larum; such one
As *folk ring bees with basins—the world run-*
        neth on wheels.
But except her maid *show a fair pair of heels,*
She haleth her by the boy rope, till her brains
        ache.   [make—
And bring I home a good dish, good cheer to
What is this? (saith she).   Good meat, (say I),
        for yow !   [sow !
God have mercy, horse! a pig of mine own
Thus when I see by kindness ease reneweth
        not,   [*reweth not;*
And then, *that the eye seeth not, the heart*
And that *he must needs go whom the devil doth*
        drive;
Her force forcing me, for mine ease to contrive
To let her fast and fret alone for me,
I go where merry chat and good cheer may be.
Much spend I abroad, which at home should
        be spent
If she would leave controlling and be content.
There leaped a whiting, (quoth she), and leaped
        in straight;   [ceit.
Take a hair from his beard, and mark this con-
He maketh you believe, by lies laid on by load,

My brawling at home maketh him banquet
    abroad.   [home.
Where his banquets abroad make me brawl at
For, as in a frost, a mud wall made of loam
Cracketh and crummeth in pieces asunder,
So melteth his money, to the world's wonder.
Thus may ye see, *to turn the cat in the pan,*
Or *set the cart before the horse*, well he can;
He is but little at home, the truth is so;
And, forth with him, he will not let me go;
And if I come to be merry where he is,
Then is he mad, as ye shall hear by this.
Where he, with gossips at a banquet late was,
At which, as use is, he paid all—but let pass!
I came to be merry; wherewith merrily:
Proface! *Have among you blind harpers,* (said
    I)—
The mo the merrier, we all day hear and see.
Yea, but *the fewer the better fare*, (said he).
Then here were, ere I came, (quoth I), too
    many;
Here is but little meat left, if there be any.
And *it is ill coming,* I have heard say,
To th' end of a shot and beginning of a fray.
Put up thy purse, (quoth he), thou shalt none
    pay;   [thy way.
And fray here should be none were thou gone
*Here is, since thou camest, too many feet
    a-bed;*   [errand sped.
Welcome! when thou goest: thus is thine
I come, (quoth I), to be one here, if I shall—
It is merry in hall when beards wag all.
What, bid me welcome, pig? I pray thee kiss
    me!
Nay, farewell, sow! (quoth he), *our Lord bliss
    me*

From *bassing of beasts of Bearbinder Lane.*
I have, (quoth I), for fine sugar, fair rat's-bane.
Many years since, my mother said to me,
Her elders would say : *it is better to be*
An old man's darling than a young man's war-
    ling.
And God knoweth ! I knew none of this snarl-
    ing
In my old husband's days; for, as tenderly
He loved me as ye love me slenderly;
We drew both in one line. Quoth he, *would*
    to our lord   [*cord.*
Ye had, in that drawing, *hanged both in one*
For I never meet thee at flesh, nor at fish,
But *I have* sure *a dead man's head in my dish;*
Whose best and my worst day, that wish might
    be,
Was when thou didst bury him and marry me.
If you, (quoth I), long for change in those
    cases,
Would to God he and you had changed places!
But best I change place, for here I may be
    spared,
And for my kind coming, this is my reward.
Claw a churl by th' arse, and he shitteth in my
    hand;   [band.
Knack me that nut, much good doyt you all this
Must she not, (quoth he), be welcome to us all,
Among us all, letting such a farewell fall?
Such carpenters, such chips, (quoth she); folk
    tell;   [*farewell.*
Such lips, such lettuce; such welcome, such
Thine own words, (quoth he), thine own wel-
    come marr'd.   [jarr'd,
Well, (said she), whensoever we twain have
My words be pried at narrowly, I espy.

Ye can see a mote in another man's eye,
But ye cannot see a balk in your own.
Yea, mark my words, but not that they be
    grown
By your revellous riding on every royle;
Well nigh every day a new mare or a moyle,
As much unhonest, as unprofitable,
Which shall bring us shortly to be *unable*
To give a dog a loaf, as I have oft said.
Howbeit, your pleasure may no time be denied,
But still you must have both the finest meat,
Apparel, and all thing that money may geat;
Like *one* of fond fancy so fine and so neat
That would have better bread than is made of
    wheat.
The best is best cheap, (quoth he), men say
    clear.
Well, (quoth she), *a man may buy gold too*
    dear;
Ye nother care, nor wellnigh cast what ye pay,
To buy the dearest for the best alway.
Then for your diet who useth feeding such,
Eat more than enough, and drink much more
    too much.   [school :
But temperance teacheth this, where he keepeth
He that knoweth when he hath enough is no
    fool.
Feed by measure, and defy the physician;
And, in the contrary, mark this condition :
A swine over fat is cause of his own bane;
Who seeth nought herein, his wit is in the
    wane.
But *pompous provision, cometh not all, alway*
Of gluttony, but of pride sometime, some say.
But this proverb preacheth to men haut or
    high :

Hew not too high lest the chips fall in thine eye.
Measure is a merry mean, as this doth show :
Not too high for the pye, nor too low for the
      crow.
The difference between staring and stark blind
The wise man at all times to follow can find;
And i-wis an auditor of a mean wit,   [yit;
May soon accompt, though hereafter come not
Yet is he sure, *be the day never so long,*
Evermore at last they ring to evensong.
And where ye spend much though ye spent but
      lickle,
Yet *little and little the cat eateth the flickle;*
Little loss by length may grow importable;
A mouse in time may bite a-two a cable.
Thus, to end of all things, be we lief or loth,
Yet lo, *the pot so long to the water goeth,*
Till at the last it cometh home broken;
Few words to the wise suffice to be spoken.
If ye were wise, here were enough, (quoth she).
Here is enough, and too much, dame, (quoth
      he);
For, though this appear a proper pulpit piece,
Yet *when the fox preacheth then beware your*
      geese.
A good tale ill told, in the telling is marred.
So are, (quoth she), good tales well told, and
      ill heard.   [*wit*, wife :
Thy tales, (quoth he), show *long hair, and short*
But long be thy legs, and short be thy life.
Pray for yourself! I am not sick, (quoth she).
Well let's see, what thy last tale cometh to,
      (quoth he) :   [wander;
Thou sayest I spend all; to this, thy words
But, *as deep drinketh the goose as the gander.*
Thou canst cough in the aumbry, if need be,

When I shall cough without bread or broth for
    thee.
Whereby, while thou sendest me abroad to
    spend,
*Thou gossipest at home to meet me at land's
    end.*   [mean—
Ah! then I beguile you, (quoth she), this ye
But sir! *my pot is whole, and my water clean.*
Well, thou wouldst have me, (quoth he), pinch
    like a snudge,
Every day to be thy drivel and drudge.
Not so, (quoth she), but I would have ye stir
Honestly; *to keep the wolf from the dur.*
I would drive the wolf out at door first, (quoth
    he);
And that can I not do, till I drive out thee.
A man were better be drowned in Venice gulf
Than have such a bearded bear, or such a wolf!
But had I not been witched, my wedding to
    flee,   [me.
The terms that long to wedding had warned
First, wooing for woeing; banna for banning;
The banns for my bane; and then this, thus
    scanning—
Marrying marring. And what married I than?
A woman! As who saith, woe to the man!
Thus wed I with woe, wed I Jill, wed I Jane—
I pray God, *the devil go with thee down the
    lane!*   [agreed),
I grant, (quoth she), this doth sound, (as ye
On your side in words, but on my side in deed.
Thou grant'st this grant, (quoth he), without
    any grace;
Ungraciously, to thy side, to turn this case.
Leave this, (quoth she), and learn liberality
To stint strife, grown by your prodigality.

                      G 2

Oft said the wise man, whom I erst did bury:
Better are meals many than one too merry.
Well, (quoth he), that is answered with this,
    wife: [*whole life.*
Better is one month's cheer than a churl's
I think it learning of a wiser lectour,
To learn to make myself mine own exectour,
Than spare for another that might wed thee,
As the fool, thy first husband, spared for me.
And as for ill places, thou seekest me in mo,
And in worse too, than I into any go.
Whereby this proverb showeth thee in by the
    week:
No man will another in the oven seek
Except that himself have been there before.
God give grace thou hast been good! I say no
    more;   [couldst prove
And would have thee say less except thou
Such process as thou slanderously dost move.
For slander, perchance, (quoth she), I not deny
It may be a slander, but it is no lie.
It is a lie, (quoth he), and thou a liar!
Will ye, (quoth she), drive me to touch ye
    nigher?   [yit
I rub the galled horse back till he winch; and
He would make it seem that I touch him no
    whit.   [make:
But I wot what I wot, though I few words
Many kiss the child for the nurse's sake.
Ye have many good children to look upon,
And ye bless them all, but ye bass but one.
This half showeth, what the whole meaneth,
    that I meve,
Ye fet circumquaques to *make me believe,*
Or think, *that the moon is made of a green*
    cheese.

And when ye have made me a lout in all these,
It seemeth ye would make me go to bed at
    noon.
Nay, (quoth he), *the day of doom shall be done*
Ere thou go to bed at noon, or night, for me.
Thou art, to be plain, and not to flatter thee,
As wholesome a morsel for my comely corse
As a shoulder of mutton for a sick horse.
The devil with his dam hath more rest in hell
Than I have here with thee; but well, wife,
    well !   [*buckets.*
Well, well ! (quoth she), *many wells, many*
Yea ! (quoth he), and *many words, many*
    buffets.   [thus,
Had you some husband, and snapped at him
Iwys he would give you a recumbentibus.
A dog will bark ere he bite, and so thou
After thy barking wilt bite me, I trow now ;
But *it is hard to make an old dog stoop,* lo !
Sir, (quoth she), *a man may handle his dog so*
That he may make him bite him, though he
    would not.   [*wives scold not ;*
Husbands are in heaven, (quoth he), *whose*
Thou makest me claw where it itcheth not. I
    would   [cold ;
Thy tongue were cooled to make thy tales more
That aspen leaf, such spiteful clapping have
    bred,
That *my cap is better at ease than my head.*
God send that head, (said she), *a better nurse !*
For *when the head acheth all the body is the*
    worse.
God grant, (quoth I), the head and body, both
    two,
To nurse each other better than they do :
Or ever have done for the most times past.

I brought to nurse both, (quoth she), had it not
    been waste.   [*meal;*
Margery, gôod cow, (quoth he), *gave a good*
But then she cast it down again with her heel.
How can her purse for profit be delightful
Whose person and properties be thus spiteful?
A piece of a kid is worth two of a cat—
Who the devil will change a rabbit for a rat?
If I might change, I would rather choose to
    beg,
Or sit with a roasted apple or an egg
Where mine appetite serveth me to be,
Than every day *to fare like a duke* with thee!
Like a duke? like a duck! (quoth she), thou
    shalt fare,   [yet spare.
Except thou wilt spare, more than thou dost
Thou farest too well, (quoth he), but *thou art*
    so wood,   [*doth thee good.*
Thou knowest not who doth thee harm, who
Yes, yes! (quoth she), for all those wise words
    uttered,
I know on which side my bread is buttered;
But *there will no butter cleave on my bread,*
And on my bread any butter·to be spread;
Every promise that thou therein dost utter,
Is *as sure as it were sealed with butter,*
Or a mouse tied with a thread. Every good
    thing
Thou lettest even slip, like a waghalter slip-
But take up in time, or else I protest, [string.
All be not a-bed that shall have ill rest.
Now, go to thy darlings, and declare thy grief,
Where all thy pleasure is: *hop whore, pipe*
    thief!

CHAPTER VIII.

With this, thence hopped she; wherewith, O
    Lord ! he cried,   [bide?
What wretch but I this wretchedness could
Howbeit, in all this woe, I have no wrong;
For it only is all on myself along.
Where *I should have bridled her first with*
    rough bit,
To have made her chew on the bridle one fit,
For lickorous lucre of a little winning,
. *I gave her the bridle at beginning;*
And now *she taketh the bridle in the teeth,*
And runneth away with it; whereby each man
    seeth
It is, (as old men right well understand),
Ill putting a naked sword in a madman's hand.
She taketh such heart of grace that though I
    maim her,
Or kill her, yet shall I never reclaim her.
She hath, (they say), been s'iff-necked ever-
    more;
And *it is ill healing of an old sore.*
This proverb prophesied many years agone :
It will not out of the flesh that is bred in the
    bone.   [sort
What chance have I, to have a wife of such
That will no fault amend, in earnest nor sport?
A small thing amiss lately I did espy,
Which to make her mend, by a jest merrily,
I said but this : *taunt tivet, wife, your nose*
    drops;
So it may fall, I will eat 'no browesse sops
This day.   But two days after this came in ure,
I had sorrow to my sops enough, be sure !

Well! (quoth I), *it is ill jesting on the sooth;*
Sooth bourd is no bourd, in ought that mirth
    doeth.
Such jests could not juggle her, were ought
    amiss,
Nor *turn melancholy to mirth*; for it is
No playing with a straw before an old cat.
Every trifling toy age cannot laugh at;
Ye may walk this way, but sure ye shall find
The further ye go, the further behind.
Ye should consider the woman is old: [*cold!*
And what for? a hot word? *soon hot, soon*
Bear with them that bear with you, and she is
    scanned
Not only *the fairest flower in your garland,*
But also she is all the fair flowers thereof:
Will ye requite her then with a taunting scoff?
Or with any other kind of unkindness? [*ness!*
Take heed is a fair thing: beware this blind-
Why will ye, (quoth he), I shall follow her will?
To make me John Drawlatch, or such a sneak-
    bill?
To bring her solace that bringeth me sorrow?
By'r lady! then *we shall catch birds to-morrow:*
A good wife maketh a <u>good</u> husband, (they
    say).
That, (quoth I), ye may turn another way:
To make a good husband, make a good wife;
I can no more herein, but *God stint all strife!*
Amen! (quoth he), and God have mercy,
    brother!
I will now mend this house and pair another.
And that he meant, of likelihood, by his own;
For, so apaired he that, ere three years were
    grown,
That little and little he decayed so long,

Till he at length *came to buckle and bare
     thong.*
To discharge charge, that necessarily grew,
There was *no more water than the ship drew.*
Such drifts drave he, *from ill to worse and
Till he was *as bare as a bird's arse.*   [*worse,*
Money, and money worth, did so miss him
That *he had not now one penny to bliss him;*
Which, foreseen in this woman, wisely weigh-
     ing   [ing,
That meet was to stay somewhat for her stay-
To keep yet one mess for Alison in store,
She kept one bag that he had not seen before :
A poor cook that may not lick his own fingers.
But about her at home now still he lingers,
*Not checker a-boord, all was not clear in the
     coast,*
He looked like one that had beshit the roast.
But whether any secret tales were sprinkling,
Or that he by guess had got an inkling
Of her hoard; or that he thought to amend,
And *turn his ill beginning to a good end*
In showing himself a new man, as was fit,
That appeared shortly after, but not yet.

CHAPTER IX.

One day in their arbour—which stood so to
     mine,
That I might, and did, closely mine ear incline,
And likewise cast mine eye, to hear and see
What they said and did, where they could not
He unto her a goodly tale began,   [see me—
More like a wooer than a wedded man.
As ferre as matter thereof therein served

But the first part from words of wooing
    swerved,
And stood upon repentance, with submission
Of his former crooked unkind condition;
Praying her to *forgive and forget* all, free
And he *forgave* her *as he forgiven would be*;
Loving her now, as he full deeply swore,
As hótly as ever he loved her before.
Well, well! (quoth she), whatever ye now say,
It is too late to call again yesterday.
Wife! (quoth he), such may my diligence seem
That th'offence of yesterday I may redeem;
God taketh me as I am, and not as I was—
Take you me so too, and let all things past
    pass.   [think plain:
I pray thee, good wife! think I speak and
What! *he runneth far that never turneth again.*
Ye be young enough to mend, I agree it;
But I am, (quoth she), too old to see it;
And amend ye or not, I am too old a year.
What is life where living is extinct clear?
Namely at old years of least help and most
    need;   [heed.
But no tale could tune you in time to take
If I tune myself now, (quoth he), it is fair;
And hope of true tune shall tune me from de-
    spair.   [(said she);
Believe well, and have well, men say; yea,
Do well, and have well, men say also, we see.
But what man can believe, that man can do
    well
Who of no man will counsel take, or hear tell?
Which to you, when any man any way tried,
Then *were ye deaf: ye could not hear on that*
    side.
Whoever with you any time therein wears,

He must *both tell you a tale, and find you ears.*
You had on your harvest ears, thick of hearing;
But this is a question of old inquiring :
Who is so deaf, or so blind, as is he
That wilfully will nother hear nor see?
When I saw your manner, my heart for woe
    molt ;   [*bolt :*
Then would ye *mend as the fletcher mends his*
Or *as sour ale mendeth in summer :* I know,
And *knew, which way the wind blew*, and will
    blow.
Though not to my profit, a prophet was I :
I prophesied this, too true a prophecy.
When I was right *ill believed, and worse hard*,
By flinging from your folks at home, which all
    marred,
When I said in semblance either cold or warm :
A man far from his good is nigh his harm.
Or willed ye to look, that ye lost no more,
On such as show that *hungry flies bite sore,*
Then would ye look over me, with stomach
Like as the devil looked over Lincoln. [swollen,
The devil is dead, wife, (quoth he), for ye see
I look like a lamb in all your words to me.
Look as ye list now, (quoth she), thus looked ye
    than ;
And for those looks I show this, to show each
    man,
Such proof of this proverb, as none is greater,
Which saith, that *some man may steal a horse*
    better
Than some other may stand and look upon.
Lewd huswives might have words, but I not
    one
That might be allowed. But now if ye look,
In mistaking me, ye may see, *ye took*

The wrong way to wood, and the wrong sow by
  th'ear;
And thereby *in the wrong box* to thrive, ye
  were.
I have heard some, to some tell this tale not
  seeld :
When thrift is in the town, ye be in the field;
But contrary, you made that sense to sown,
When thrift was in the field, ye were in the
  town.   [any;
Field ware might *sink or swim* while ye had
Town ware was your ware *to turn the penny.*
But town or field, where most thrift did appear,
What ye won in the hundred ye lost in the
  shire—
In all your good husbandry thus rid the rock.
Ye stumbled at a straw, and leapt over a block.
So many kinds of increase you had in choice,
And nought increase nor keep, how can I re-
  joice?
Good riding at two anchors men have told,
For if the tone fail, the tother may hold.
But you leave all anchor hold, on seas or lands,
And so *set up shop upon Goodwin's sands.*
But as folk have a saying, both old and true,
In that they say : *black will take none other*
So may I say here, to my deep dolour, [*hue;*
It is a bad cloth that will take no colour.
This case is yours; for ye were never so wise
To take speck of colour of good advice.
Th'advice of all friends I say, one and other
Went in at the tone ear, and out at the tother.
And as those words went out, this proverb in
  came :
He that will not be ruled by his own dame
Shall be ruled by his stepdame; and so you,

Having lost your own good, and own friends
  now,
May seek your foreign friends, if you have any.
And sure one of my great griefs, among many,
Is that ye have been so very a hog   [*dog!*
To my friends.   What, man? *love me, love my*
But you, *to cast precious stones before hogs,*   ⎯
Cast my good before a sort of cur dogs
And salt bitches; which by whom now de-
  voured,
And your honesty among them deflowered,
And that you may no more expense afford,
Now can they not afford you one good word,
And you them as few.   And old folk under-
  stood :   [*good.*
When thieves fall out true men come to their
Which is not alway true; for, in all that bretch,
I can no farthing of my good the more fetch;
Nor, I trow, themselves neither, if they were
  sworn ;
Light come, light go! And sure, since we were
  born,
Ruin of one ravine was there none greater;
For, by your gifts, they be as little the better
As you be much the worse, and I cast away—
An ill wind that bloweth no man to good, men
  say.   [*the corn.*
Well, (quoth he), *every wind bloweth not down*
I hope, (I say), *good hap be not all outworn.*
I will now begin thrift, when thrift seemeth
  gone—   [*than one :*
What, wife! *there be mo ways to the wood*
And I will assay all the ways to the wood
Till I find one way to get again this good.
Ye will get it again, (quoth she), I fear,
As shortly as a horse will lick his ear.

The Dutchman sayeth, that *segging is good
    cope;*
Good words bring not ever of good deeds good
    hope;   ·   [scorn—
And these words show your words spoken in
It pricketh betimes that will be a good thorn;
*Timely crooketh the tree, that will a good
    cammock be.*
And, *such beginning such end,* we all day see;
And you, by me at beginning being thriven,
And then to keep thrift could not be pricked nor
    driven—
How can ye now get thrift, the stock being
    gone?
Which is th'only thing to rise thrift upon.
Men say: *he may ill run that cannot go,*
And your gain, without your stock, runneth
    even so.
For, *what is a workman without his tools?*—
Tales of Robin Hood are good among fools.
He can ill pipe that lacketh his upper lip;
*Who lacketh a stock, his gain is not worth a
    chip.*
A tale of a tub, your tale no truth avoweth;
*Ye speak now as ye would creep into my
    mouth;*
In pure painted process—*as false as fair*—
How ye will amend when ye cannot appair?
But against gay glossers this rude text re-
    cites:
It is not all butter that the cow shites.
I heard once a wise man say to his daughter:
Better is the last smile than the first laughter.
We shall, I trust, (quoth he), laugh again at
    last,
Although I be once out of the saddle cast;

Yet, since I am bent to sit, this will I do :
Recover the horse or lese the saddle too. [hap,
Ye never could yet, (quoth she), recover any
To win or save ought, to stop any one gap.
For stopping of gaps, (quoth he), care not a
    rush,
I will learn *to stop two gaps with one bush.*
Ye will, (quoth she), as soon *stop gaps with*
    rushes   .
As with any husbandly handsome bushes.
Your tales have like taste, where temperance is
    taster,
To *break my head, and then give me a plaster.*
Now thrift is gone, now would ye thrive in all
    haste ;   [*waste.*
And when ye had thrift, ye had *like haste to*
Ye liked then better an inch of your will
Than an ell of your thrift. Wife (quoth he),
    be still,
May I be holp forth an inch at a pinch,
I will yet thrive, (I say): *As good is an inch*
As an ell. Ye can, (quoth she), make it so
    well ;
For when *I gave you an inch, ye took an ell,*
Till both ell and inch be gone, and we in debt.
Nay, (quoth he), *with a wet finger* ye can fet
As much as may easily all this matter ease ;
And this debate also pleasantly appease. [now,
I could do as much with an hundred pound
As with a thousand afore, I assure you.
Yea, (quoth she), *who had that he hath not*
    would
Do that he doeth not, as old men have told.
Had I, as ye have, I would do more, (quoth
    he),   [see.
Than the priest spake of on Sunday, ye should

Ye do, as I have, (quoth she); for nought I
    have
And nought ye do.   What, man! I trow ye
    rave: [*cake?*
Would ye both *eat your cake and have your*
Ye have had of me all that I might make;
And, *be a man never so greedy to win,*
He can have no more of the fox but the skin.
Well! (quoth he), if ye list to bring it out,
Ye can give me your blessing in a clout.
That were for my child, (quoth she), had I
    ony;
But husband! I have neither child, nor money.
Ye cast and conjecture this much, like in show,
As the blind man casts his staff, or shoots the
    crow.   [none,
Howbeit, had I money right much, and ye
Yet to be plain, ye should have none for Joan.
Nay, he that first flattereth me, as ye have
    done,
And doth as ye did to me after, so soon,
He may be in my Pater noster indeed;
But be sure, he shall never come in my Creed.
Ave Maria! (quoth he), how much motion
Here is to prayers, with how little devotion;
But some men say : *no penny no Pater noster!*
I say to such (said she): *no longer foster,*
No longer lemman.   But fare and well then,
Pray and shift each one for himself, as he can:
Every man for himself, and God for us all.
To those words he said nought; but, forthwith
    did fall   [speech.
From *harping on that string* to fair flattering
And, as I erst said, he did her so beseech,
That things *erst so far off* were *now so far on,*
That as she may wallow, away she is gone

Where all that was left lay with a trusty friend,
Dwelling a good walk from her at the town's
    end.
And back again straight a halting pace she
    hobbles,
Bringing a bag of royals and nobles;
All that she had, without restraint of one jot—
She brought bullock's noble, for noble or groat
Had she not one mo: which I after well knew.
And anon smiling, toward him as she drew,
Ah, sir! *light burden far heavy* (quoth she);
This light burden in long walk well-nigh trieth
    me.
God give grace I play not the fool this day;
For here *I send th'axe after the helve away.*
But if ye will stint and avoid all strife,
Love and cherish this as ye would my life.
I will, (quoth he), wife, by God Almighty!
This gear *cometh* even *in pudding time rightly.*
He snatched at the bag. *No haste but good,*
    (quoth she);
Short shooting leseth your game, ye may see.
Ye missed the cushion, for all your haste to it,
And *I may set you beside the cushion yit,*
And *make you wipe your nose upon your sleeve*
For ought ye shall win without ye axe me leave.
Have ye not heard tell, *all covet, all lose?*
Ah, sir! I see *ye may see no green cheese*
But your teeth must water—a good cockney
    coke!
Though ye love not *to buy the pig in the poke,*
Yet snatch ye at the poke, that the pig is in,
Not for the poke, but the pig good cheap to
    win.
Like one half lost, till greedy grasping gat it,
Ye would be over the stile ere ye come at it.

But abide, friend! *your mother bid till ye were
    born:*   [morn.
Snatching winneth it not, if ye snatch till to
Men say, (said he), *long standing and small
    offering*   [proffering
Maketh poor persons; and, in such signs and
Many pretty tales and merry toys had they,
Before this bag came fully from her away.
Kindly he kissed her, with words not tart nor
    tough :   [enough.
But *the cat knoweth whose lips she licketh well*
Anon, the bag she delivered him, and said
He should bear it, for that it now heavy
    weighed.
With good will, wife! for it is, (said he to her),
*A proud horse that will not bear his own pro-
    vender.*
And oft before seemed she never so wise,
Yet was she now, suddenly waxen *as nice
As it had been a halporth of silver spoons.*
Thus *cloudy mornings turn to clear afternoons*;
But so nigh noon it was, that by and by,
They rose, and went to dinner lovingly.

CHAPTER X.

This dinner thought he long, and straight after
To his accustomed customers he gat;   [that
With whom, in what time he spent one groat
    before,
In less time he spent now ten groats or more;
And in small time he brought the world so
    about   [out.
That *he brought the bottom of the bag clean*
His gadding thus again made her ill content;

But she not so much as dreamed that all was
    spent.
Howbeit, suddenly, she minded on a day
To pick the chest lock, wherein this bag lay;
Determining this : if it lay whole still,
So shall it lie—no mite she minish will; [best
And, if the bag began to shrink, she thought
To take for her part some part of the rest.
But straight as she had forthwith opened the
    lock,
And looked in the bag *what it was a clock,*
Then was it proved true, as this proverb goeth :
He that cometh last to the pot is soonest wroth.
By her coming last, and too late to the pot,
Whereby she was *potted* thus *like a sot*
To see the pot both skimmed for running over,
And also all the liquor run at rover.
At her good husband's and her next meeting,
The devil's good grace might have given a
    greeting,
Either for honour or honesty, as good [wood ;
As she gave him : she was, (as they say), horn
In no place could she sit herself to settle,
It seemed to him *she had pissed on a nettle.*
She nettled him, and he rattled her so,
That at end of that fray asunder they go;
And never after came together again—
He turned her out at doors to graze on the
    plain,
And himself went after; for, within fortnight,
All that was left was launched out quite.
And *thus had he brought haddock to paddock,*
Till they both were *not worth a haddock.*
It hath been said : *need maketh the old wife*
    trot—
Other folk said it, but she did it, God wot !

First from friend to friend, and then from dur
    to dur,
A-begging of some that had begged of her.
But as men say : *misery may be mother*
Where one beggar is driven to beg of another.
And thus wore and wasted this most woeful
    wretch,   [fetch.
Till death from this life did her wretchedly
Her late husband, and now widower, here and
    there   [where;
Wandering about, *few know and fewer care*
Cast out as an abject, he leadeth his life
Till famine belike fet him after his wife.
  Now let us note here : First, of the first
    twain,
Where they both wedded, together to remain,
Hoping joyful presence should wear out all
    woe :
Yet *poverty brought that joy to joy*-fail, lo !
But, notably note these last twain : whereas he
Took her only for that he rich would be,
And she him only in hope of good hap
In her doting days to be danced on the lap.
In condition they differed so many ways,
That lightly *he laid her up for holy days;*
Her good he laid up so, lest thieves might spy
    it,
That nother she could, nor he can, come by it.
Thus failed all four, of all things less and
    more,
Which they all, or any of all, married for.

CHAPTER XI.

Forsooth ! said my friend, *this matter maketh boast*
Of diminution. For, *here is a mill post*
Thwitten to a pudding prick so nearly,
That I confess me discouraged clearly.
In both my weddings, in all things, except one,
This spark of hope have I, to proceed upon :
Though these and some other speed ill as ye
    tell,
Yet other have lived and loved full well.
If I should deny that, (quoth I), I should rave ;
For, of both these sorts, I grant, that myself
    have
Seen of the tone sort, and heard of the tother,
That liked and lived right well, each with
    other.
But whether fortune will you that man declare,
That shall choose in this choice, your comfort
    or care,
Since, before ye have chosen, we cannot know,
I thought to lay the worst, as ye the best show,
That ye might, being yet at liberty,
With all your joy, join all your jeopardy.
And now, in this heard, in these cases on each
    part,
I say no more, but *lay your hand on your heart.*
I heartily thank you, (quoth he) ; *I am sped*
Of mine errand : this hitteth the nail on the
    head.
Who that leaveth surety and leaneth unto
    chance,
When fools pipe, by authority *he may dance.*
And sure am I, of those twain, if I none choose,

Although I nought win, yet shall I nought
    lose.
And to win a woman here, and lose a man,
In all this great winning what gain win I
    than?
But, mark how folly hath me away carried;
How, like a weathercock, I have here varied:
First, these two women to lose I was so loth,
That if I might, I would have wedded them
    both;   [them;
Then thought I since, to have wedded one of
And, now know I clear, I will wed none of
    them.
They both shall have this one answer by letter:
As good never a whit as never the better.
Now let me ask, (quoth I), and yourself
    answer
The short question that I asked while're.
A foul, old, rich widow, whether wed would ye,
Or a young, fair maid, being poor as ye be?
In neither barrel better herring, (quoth he).
I like thus richesse as ill as poverty;
Who that hath either of these pigs in ure,
He hath *a pig of the worse pannier* sure.
I was wedded unto my will; howbeit,
I will be devorst, and be wed to my wit;
Whereby, with these examples past, I may
    see
Fond wedding, for love, as good only to flee.
Only for love, or only for good,
Or only for both I wed not, by my hood!
Thus, no one thing only, though one thing
    chiefly
Shall woo me to wed now: for now I espy,
Although the chief one think in wedding be
    love,

Yet must mo things join, as all in one may
    move
Such kind of living, for such kind of life,
As lacking the same, *no lack to lack a wife.*
Here is enough, I am satisfied, (said he).
Since *enough is enough,* (said I), here may we,
With that one word take end good, as may be
    guessed
For folk say : *enough is as good as a feast.*

Finis.

A NOTE-BOOK, WORD-LIST, AND INDEX

INCLUDING

REFERENCES, NOTES, A COMPLETE INDEX TO ALL THE PROVERBS, PROVERBIAL SAYINGS, COLLOQUIALISMS, &c., together with a GLOSSARY OF WORDS AND PHRASES now Archaic or Obsolete; the whole arranged in ONE ALPHABET IN DICTIONARY FORM

A FOREWORD TO NOTE-BOOK, WORD-LIST, AND INDEX

Reference from text to Note-Book is copious, and as complete as may be; so also, conversely, from Note-Book to text. The following pages may, with almost absolute certainty, be consulted on any point that may occur in the course of reading.

The scheme of reference from Note-Book to text assumes the division, in the mind's eye, of each page into four horizontal sections; which, beginning at the top, are indicated in the Note-Book by the letters a, b, c, d following the page figure. In practice this will be found easy, and an enormous help to the eye over the usual reference to page alone in "fixing" the "catchword." Thus 126a = the first quarter of page 126; 40c = the third quarter of page 40; and so forth.

The Index to the Proverbs, Proverbial Sayings, Colloquialisms, &c., is given with much completeness. "Epigrams" (as a reference) = found also in "The Epigrams on Proverbs": see Heywood, Works, II. (E.E.D.S.).

NOTE-BOOK, WORD-LIST,
AND INDEX

To John Heywood's Proverbs concerning Marriage

ABJECT, "cast out as an abject" (100*b*), vagabond, ne'er-do-well, despicable person. "I deemed it better so to die, Than at my foeman's feet an abject lie."—*Mirrour for Magistrates* (1599), 20.

ABROOD, "weather meet to set paddocks abrood in" (50*b*), *i.e.* weather fit for toads or frogs to be abroad: cf. "fine weather for ducks."

ABSENTETH, "her presence absenteth all maladies" (10*c*), makes absent, expels, cures: now always with the reflective pronouns. ". . . or what change Absents thee or what chance detains?"—Milton, *Par. Lost* (bk. x.).

ACCOMPTE, "the full accompte" (8*d*), account: the old spelling. "*Smith.* The clerk of Chatham: he can write and read, and caste accompt."—Shakspeare, 2 *Henry VI.* (1594), iv. 2.

ADVOUTRY, "in advoutry to catch him" (71*b*), adultery. "Calling this match advoutrie, as it was."—*Mirrour for Magistrates* (1599), 342.

AGE, "age and appetite fell at strong strife" (51*d*).

ALE, (*a*) "when ale is in wit is out" (Epig.).
(*b*) "as sour ale mendeth in summer" (91*b*), that is, not at all.

ALE-CLOUT, "wash her face in an ale-clout" (26*d*), get drunk.

AM, "God taketh me as I am and not as I was" (90*b*).

AMATED, " all mirth was amated " (17*d*), paralysed, checked.

AMENDMENT, " let your amendment amend the matter " (77*a*).

AN, see And.

ANCHOR, (*a*) " I will straight weigh anchor and hoist up sail " (21*c*).

(*b*) " good riding at two anchors, For if the one fail, the t'other may hold " (92*c*), best to have more chances than one : cf. " two strings to one's bow."

AND, AN (*passim*), (*a*) if ; (*b*) on.

ANGRY, (*a*) " he that will be angry without cause, must be at one, without amends " (61*c*).

(*b*) " if she be angry, beshrew her angry heart " (44*d*).

APAIRED, " so apaired he " (88*d*), grew worse, degenerated. " I see the more that I them forbear, The worse they be from year to year : All that liveth appaireth fast."—*Everyman* (E.E.D.S., *Anon. Plays*, 1st Ser., 94*d*).

APARTY, " choose we him aparty " (67*s*), aside, separate. " He that es verrayly meke, God sal safe hym of there, here aparty, and in tother worlde plenerly."—*MS. Coll. Eton.* 10, f. 40.

APE, (*a*) " she can no more harm than can a she ape " (27*d*).

(*b*) " the dun ape hath trod on both thy feet " (Epig.).

(*c*) As a verb, *ape* = to befool or dupe ; also, *to make one an ape*.

APPETITE, " age and appetite fell at strong strife " (51*d*).

APPLE, " lost with an apple and won with a nut " (24*b*). " Nor woman true, but even as stories tell, Won with an egg, and lost again with shell."—Gascoigne, *Ferdinando* (d. 1577).

ASHES, " raked up in th' ashes and covered again " (58*b*).

ASPEN-LEAF, " thy tongue that aspen-leaf " (85*c*).

ASSAY, " I will assay to win some favour " (21d), endeavour, try, essay. " Yet wol I make assay."— Chaucer, *Cant. Tales* (1383), 13177.

ASSURANCE, " words of assurance " (5d), affiance, betrothal. " This druge, diviner laid claim to me; called me Dromio; swore I was assured to her."— Shakspeare, *Comedy of Errors* (1593), iii. 2.

AUDRY, see Saint Audry.

AVAIL, " avail, unhappy hook " (44a), *i.e.* Away! Begone! you are defeated in your purpose; *hook*=a term of reproach. " That unhappy hook."—*Jack Juggler* (E.E.D.S., *Anon. Plays*, Ser. 3), 26c and 35d.

AVANCED, " which should me much avanced " (22a), profited, advanced.

AXE, " I send th' axe after helve away " (97b), *i.e.* I despair; " In for a penny, in for a pound."

(b), " without ye axe me leave " (97c), ask: the word and also the construction, once literary, are now vulgar.

BACHELORS, (a) " bachelors boast how they will teach their wives good " (74d), hence bachelor's wife=an ideal wife: see *infra*.
(b) " bachelors' wives and maids' children be well taught " (75a). " The maid's child is ever best taught."—Latimer, *Sermons* (1562), v. " Ay, ay, bachelors' wives, indeed, are finely governed."— Vanbrugh, *Provoked Wife* (1726), i. 1.

BACKARE, " Backare, quoth Mortimer to his sow " (41c), *i.e.* " Go back," " Give place," " Away ": the allusion is lost, though the phrase is common enough in old writers, the earliest dating about 1473.

BAG, " he brought the bottom of the bag clean out " (98d), to make an end of things, to tell all, to lose all.

BAKER, " so late met, that I fear we part not yet, quoth the baker to the pillory " (57b), severe penalties for impurity of bread or shortness of weight were enforced against bakers from very early times; they were frequently the subject of much sarcasm. " A pillorie for the punishment of bakers, offending in the assize of bread."—Stow, *Survey* (1598), 208. " They say the owl was a baker's *daughter.*"—Shakspeare, *Hamlet* (1602), iv. 5. "Are not bakers' armes the skales of Iustice? yet is not their bread light."—Dekker, *Honest Whore* (1604). "Three dear years will raise a baker's daughter to a portion. 'Tis not the smallness of the bread, but the knavery of the baker."—Ray,*Proverbs.*

BALD, "bald as a coot" (13*d*), as bald as may be: the frontal plate of the coot is destitute of feathers (see Tyndale, *Works*, 1530, ii. 224).

BALE, "this rather bringeth bale than boot" (63*d*), *bale* =trouble, sorrow; *boot*=help, cure, relief. "God send every man boot of his bale."—Chaucer, *Cant. Tales* (1483), 13409.

BALL, "thou hast stricken the ball under the line" (42*b*), *i.e.* a line regarded as marking the limit of legitimate or successful play. "Poor mortals are so many balls, Toss'd some o'er line, some under fortune's walls."—Howell, *Letters* (1645).

BANNING, "be as be may is no banning" (53*d*).

BARGAINS, "some bargains dear bought good cheap would be sold" (19*c*), *cheap*=market: *good cheap*= bon marché. "He buys other men's cunning good cheap in London, and sells it deare in the country."— Dekker, *Belman's Night Walk* (1608).

BARREL, "in neither barrel better herring" (102*c*), not a pin to choose between six of one and half a dozen of the other; elliptical—no one barrel contains herrings better than another. "Lyke Lord, lyke chaplayne, neyther barrel better herynge."—Bale, *Kynge John.* "Begin where you will, you shall find them all alike, never a barrell the better herring."—Burton, *Anat. Melan.* (1621).

BASS, to cuddle, snuggle up to; also to give a smacking kiss: once literary. "I lye *bassing* with Besse."— *Works*, 557. "Thy knees bussing the stones."— Shakspeare, *Coriol.* (1610), iii. 2.

BAUDRY, "suspicion of their baudry" (73*d*), wantonness, lechery.

BAYARD, "to have kept Bayard in the stable" (47*c*). See Blind Bayard.

BE, (*a*) " be as be may is no banning " (53*b*).

(*b*) " that shall be, shall be " (53*b*). See Shall be.

BEAD-ROLL, " a bead-roll to unfold " (77*b*), a story, narration ; specifically (as here) a catalogue of woes : properly a list of those for whom a certain number of prayers were offered, the count being kept by the telling of beads.

BEERPOT, " she was made like a beerpot or a barrel " (52*a*), well rounded in the stomach, corpulent.

BESHREW, generally in imperative. " Beshrew your heart "=woe to you. " I beshrew all shrews."— Shakspeare, *Love Labour Lost* (1594), v. 2.

BEAN, (*a*) " a bean in a monk's hood " (76*c*).

(*b*) " begging of her booteth not the worth of a bean " (30*a*), a standard of the smallest value.

BEAUTIFUL, " my beautiful marriage " (8*b*), *i.e.* marriage for beauty's sake.

BECK, " a beck as good as a dieu gard " (29*d*), nod, salutation. " Nods and becks and wreathèd smiles." —Milton, *L'Allegro* (1637).

BEFORNE (*passim*), before.

BENCHWHISTLER (37*c*), loafer, idler on an ale-house bench.

BESTILL, " a good bestill is worth a groat " (68*c*), *bestail*=a law term for all kinds of cattle : Fr., *bétail*.

BEWRAYED, " things . . . might be bewrayed " (65*b*), spoilt, muddled, complicated.

BIRD, (*a*) " better one bird in hand than ten in the wood " (36*d*), possession is everything ; hazard of loss is not worth uncertain gain : the modern version, " two in the *bush*," is not so exacting. Fr., *Mieux vaux un tenez, que deux vous l'aurez.*" " An old proverb maketh with this which I take good. Better one bird in hand then ten in the wood."—Heywood, *Witty and Witless* (*c.* 1530), *Works* (E.E.D.S.) I., 213*b*.

(*b*) " it is a foul bird that fileth his own nest " (70*d*), *fileth*=defileth : the proverb occurs as early as 1250 in *The Owl and the Nightingale*. " Rede and

lerne ye may, Howe olde proverbys say, that byrd ys
nat honest, That fylyth hys owne nest."—Skelton,
Garnesche (1520).

(c) " as bare as a bird's arse " (89a), as bare as
may be.

(d) " the birds were flown " (47d).

(e) " when birds shall roost . . . who shall appoint
their hour, the cock or hen? " (56b); compare " He
who pays the piper may call the tune."

(f) " we shall catch birds to-morrow " (88c).

BLAB, " look what she knoweth, blab it wist and out
it must " (24a), *i.e.* anything a blab knows must be
told. " Labbe hyt whyste and owt yt muste."—*MS.
Harleian* (c. 1490).

BLACK, " black will take none other hue " (92c).

BLACK OX, " the black ox never trod on thy foot " (17c),
the black ox is the symbol of decrepitude or mis-
fortune. " Venus waxeth old: and then she was a
pretie wench, when Juno was a young wife; now
crowes foote is on her eye, and the black oxe hath
trod on her foot."—Lyly, *Sapho* (1584).

BLE, " to cry ble " (34c), *ble*=bleat, as a sheep. One
of the *Hundred Mery Tales* (c. 1525) is entitled " Of
the husbande that cryed ble under the bed."

BLEED, " here doth all lie and bleed " (68c).

BLESS, " ye bless them all, but ye bass but one " (84d),
see Children.

BLESSING, " ye can give me your blessing in a clout "
(96b), *i.e.* the hoard (or talent) wrapped up in a
napkin, bag, or " stocking."

BLIND, (a) " who so deaf or so blind as is he that wilfully will never hear nor see? " (91a).

(b) " the blind eat many flies " (73b). " The blinde
eateth many a flye: So doth the husband often, iwis,
Father the childe that is not his."—*Schole-house of
Women* (1541), line 333.

(c) " blind men should judge no colours " (73a).

(d) " as the blind man casts his staff or shoots the
crow " (96b).

(e) " where the blind leadeth the blind both fall in
the dyke " (67b). " She hath hem in such wise

daunted. That they were, as who saith, enchaunted;
And as the blinde an other ledeth, And till they falle
nothing dredeth."—Gower, *Confessio Amantis.*

(*f*) " folk ofttimes are most blind in their own
cause " (73*a*), or, as in modern phrase, " blind to one's
own interests."

(*g*) " the difference between staring and stark
blind, The wise man at all times to follow can find "
(82*a*).

BLIND BAYARD, " who so bold as blind Bayard is? "
(19*d*), applied where persons act without consideration
or reflection; generic for blindness, ignorance, and
recklessness. It occurs in *The Vision of Piers the
Ploughman* (1362), and in Chaucer's *Canterbury
Tales* (1383). *Bayard* originally = a grey horse; afterwards generic; and Skelton mentions a description of
horse-loaf called " Bayard's bun." Bayard was a
horse famous in old romances; in Ariosto's great work
is called Baiardo. See Bayard.

BLISS, (*a*) " our Lord bliss me " (79*d*)—" not one penny
to bliss him " (89*a*), bless.

(*b*) see Branch.

BLIST, " by God's blist " (29*d*), bliss, joy, happiness.

BLOCKS, " I have more blocks in his way to lay " (70*a*).
obstructions, hindrances, impediments.

BOAST, (*a*) " this matter maketh boast of diminution '
(101*a*), *to make boast* = to promise well, to seem very
likely. " Nought trow I the triumphe of Julius, Of
which that Lukan maketh moche bost."—Chaucer,
Cant. Tales (1383), 4820-21.

(*b*) " Great boast and small roast Maketh unsavoury mouths wherever men host " (36*c*), *i.e.* large
promise and little performance is little to one's liking:
host = lodge, abide.

BODY, (*a*) " the big part of her body is her bum " (24*c*).
(*b*) see Leg.

BOLT, (*a*) " mend, as the thatcher mends his bolt "
(91*a*).

(*b*) see Fool.

BONGRACE (52a), a forehead cloth, or covering for the head; a kind of veil attached to a hood: afterwards the hood itself. " Her bongrace which she wore."— Heywood, *Pardoner and Frere, Works* (E.E.D.S.), I. 7c.

BOORD, " in earnest or boord " (47d), jest, joke, mock, sport. " Speak but in bord."—Udall, *Roister Doister* (1550), 75d (E.E.D.S., *Works*). See also Bourd.

BOOT, " it booteth not the worth of a bean " (30a), remedy, cure, help, advantage. " This knight thinketh his boot thou may'st be."—*Calisto and Melibœa* (E.E.D.S., *Anon Pl.*, 1st Ser.).

BORAGE, " a leaf of borage might buy all the substance that they can sell " (25c), *i.e.* just such a trifle as would be a leaf of borage in a salad, as a pot-herb, or as an ingredient in cool tankards.

BORROW, (a) " not so good to borrow as to be able to lend " (25d).
(b) " till liberty was borrow " (27c), pledged, mort-gaged. " To borrow man's soul from blame."— *World and Child* (c. 1500), E.E.D.S., *Anon. Pl.*, Ser. I., 186b.

BOSOM, " she speaketh as she would creep into your bosom " (23d).

BOUGET, " in her bouget " (75b), budget, bag, (and figuratively) store. " With that out of his bouget forth he drew Great store of treasure, therewith him to tempt."—Spenser, *Fairy Queen* (1590), III. x. 29.

BOUND, " they that are bound must obey " (68b).

BOURD, " sooth bourd is no bourd " (88a), *i.e.* a jest spoken in earnest is no jest at all; *sooth*=earnest, *bourd*=a jest: see Boord. " As the old saying is, sooth boord is no boord."—Harrington, *Briefe Apolo-gie of Poetrie* (1591).

BOW, (a) " a bow long bent, at length must wear weak " (34c), *i.e.* a bow drawn back to the utmost and often: hence " to the top of one's bent " (see also next entry).
(b) " the bent of your . . . bow " (37a), inclina-tion, tendency, disposition, course of action.

(c) " Many strings to the bow " (37a), alternatives, more resources than one. " I am wel pleased to take any coulor to defend your honor, and hope that you wyl remember, that who seaketh two stringes to one bowe, the may shute strong, but never strait."— *Letter of Queen Elizabeth to James VI*. (June, 1585).

(d) see Break.

BOWL, " this seven years, day and night to watch a bowl " (71c), *seven years* = a long time (generic) : *i.e.* may watch his coming and going a long time without discovering anything.

Box, " in the wrong box " (92a), mistaken, embarrassed, in jeopardy. " Sir, quoth I, if you will hear how St. Augustine expoundeth that place, you shall perceive that you are in a wrong box."—Ridley (" Foxe," 1838), vi. 438 (1554).

BOY ROPE, " haleth her by the boy rope " (78b), ? *bow-rope* = either, (a) the rope attached to an ox-bow ; (b) a rope of bow-string hemp ; or (c) bow-string.

BRAIN, " bitten to the brain " (45c), drunk : cf. " hair of the dog that bit one."

BRANCH, " ere . . . branch of bliss could reach any root the flower . . . faded " (17c).

BRAWLING, " brawling booteth not " (57c), *i.e.* tends to no advantage : *booteth* = profiteth.

BREAD, (a) " one . . . that would have better bread than is made of wheat " (81b).

(b) " know on which side bread is buttered " (86c), recognise one's interests : whence *to butter one's bread on both sides* = to seek advantages from more sides than one.

(c) " better is half a loaf than no bread " (37c), the earliest known example of this proverb.

(d) see Sheep's flesh.

BREAK, (a) " better is to bow than break " (22a). An early example is found in *The Morale Proverbs of Cristyne;* originally written in French about the year 1390 and of which a verse translation by Earl Rivers was printed by Caxton in 1478 : " Rather to bowe than breke is profitable, Humylite is a thing commendable."

(b) " in that house . . . a man shall as soon break his neck as his fast " (40c).

BREECH, (a) " there is nothing more vain than to beg a breech of a bare-arsed man " (20c).

(b) " the master weareth no breech " (58c; also in *Epigrams*), is not master : *to wear the breeches* =to usurp a husband's prerogative (of women). " All women be suche, Thoughe the man bere the breeche, They wyll be ever checkemate."—*Boke of Mayd Emlyn* (1515).

BRETCH, " in all that bretch " (93b), breach, quarrel, source of dissension.

BREW, " as I . . . brew, so must I . . . drink " (19a), in allusion to cause and effect. " If you have browen wel, you shal drinke the better."—Wodroephe, *Spared Houres of a Souldier* (1623).

BRIDAL (15b), a note as to the origin of the word may not be without interest. (a) " There were bride-ales, church-ales, clerk-ales, give-ales, lamb-ales, leet-ales, Midsummer-ales, Scot-ales, Whitsun-ales, and several more."—Brand's *Popular Antiquities.*

(b) " it is meet that a man be at his own bridal " (15b), a variant of " every man must attend his own funeral."

BRIDLE, (a) " I gave her the bridle at beginning " (87b), let her have her own way.

(b) " she taketh the bridle in the teeth and runneth away with it " (87b), the modern version alters " bridle " to " bit."

BRIDLED, " I should have bridled her first with rough bit, To have made her chew on the bridle one fit " (87b), *fit* =a portion or bout of anything—stanza of a song, stave of a tune, scene of a play, round at fisti-cuffs : here=a space of time.

BRIKE, " ye brike all from her, that brought all to you " (76a), *brike* =breach, violation of, or injury done to, anyone : hence deplete, " suck dry " (of money and goods).

BRIM, " better spare at brim than at bottom " (66c). *i.e.* at the beginning rather than at the end of one's tether.

BROID, " better dissemble . . . than to broid him with it " (69b), braid, abraid, reproach.

BROOM, " the green new broom sweepeth clean " (54a), still proverbial ; in the *Epigrams* " new broom sweepeth clean " is nearer the modern version.

BROTHER, " I will not trust him though he were my brother " (40c).

BUCKLE, " till he at length came to buckle and bare thong " (89a), poverty, distress : *thong*=shoestring.

BUD, " This bud sheweth what fruit will follow " (26b).

BUG, " bug's words " (66c), swaggering or threatening language ; also " bugbear words " ; of " such bugbear thoughts " (Locke). *Bug*=an object of terror, bogey. " Matrimony hath euer been a blacke bugge in their sinagoge and churche."—Bale, *Votaryes* (Pref.).

BULLOCK'S-NOBLE (97a), see Noble.

BURDEN, " light burden far heavy " (97b).

BURR, (a) " I take her for a rose, but she breedeth a burr " (26b).
    (b) " they cleave together like burrs " (72b).

BUSH, (a) " while I . . . beat the bush . . . other men . . . catch the birds " (9a). Henry the Fifth is reported to have uttered this proverb at the siege of Orleans, when the citizens, besieged by the English, declared themselves willing to yield the town to the Duke of Burgundy, who was in the English camp. " Shall I beat the bush, and another take the bird? " said King Henry. The Duke was so offended that he withdrew his troops and concluded a peace. " I beat the bush, and others catch the bird, Reason exclaimes and sweares my hap is hard."—Pettowe, *Philochasander and Elanira* (1599).
    (b) see Bird.

BUTTER, (a) " there will no butter cleave on my bread " (86c), *i.e.* nothing by which to profit or advantage.
    (b) " it is not all butter that the cow shits " (94d).
    (c) " she looketh as butter would not melt in her mouth " (27b), in contempt of persons of simple demeanour. " A cette parolle mist dame Mehault ses mains à ses costez et en grant couroux luy respondy

que . . . et que, Dieu merci, aincores fondoit le burre en sa bouche, combien qu'elle ne peust croquier noisettes, car elle n'avoit que un seul dent."—*Les Evangiles des Quenouilles (c.* 1475).

(*d*) " As sure as it were sealed with butter " (86*c*), shaky, uncertain.

BUTTERED, see Bread.

BUY, (*a*) " you to buy and sell " (23*d*), betray, impose upon.

(*b*) see Borage.

BY AND BY (50*a, et passim*), immediately, forthwith.

CAKE, " would ye both eat your cake and have your cake? " (96*a*).

CALL, " things past my hands I cannot call again " (26*a*).

CALLET (70*b*), scold, drab, trull. " A wisp of straw were worth a thousand crowns, To make this shameless callet know herself—Helen of Greece was fairer far than thou."—Shakspeare, 3 *Henry VI.* (1592), ii. 2.

CALVES, " change of pasture maketh fat calves " (62*a*). " *Boniface.* You may see what change of pasture is able to do. *Honeysuckle.* It makes fat calves in Romney Marsh, and lean knaves in London, therefore, Boniface, keep your ground."—Dekker and Webster, *Westward Hoe* (1607).

CAN, " I can some skill " (12*a*), know, able, possess. " Though he be ignorant and can little skill."—*Four Elements (c.* 1510), E.E.D.S., *Anon Pl.,* Ser. I., 3*c*.

CANDLE, (*a*) " to set up a candle before [or hold a candle to] the devil " (24*d*), to propitiate through fear, to assist in, or wink at, wrong-doing. " Though not for hope of good, yet for the feare of euill, Thou maist find ease so proffering up a candell to the deuill."—Tusser, *Husbandrie* (1557), 148.

(*b*) " upright as a candle standeth in the socket " (52*b*), as erect as may be.

(*c*) " who that worst may shall hold the candle " (56*d*).

CANSTICK, " coll under canstick " (24b), coll=(a) kiss, embrace, or (b), deceit : see Coleprophet ; canstick= candlestick. There was, however, a Christmas game called " coll under canstick."

CAP, " my cap is better at ease than my head " (85d).

CARDS, " tell thy cards and then tell me what thou hast won " (36b).

CARRAIN, " her carrain carcase " (56c), rotten, withered : a generic reproach.

CARRIER, " I will send it him by John Long the carrier " (35d), see John Long.

CARPENTER, " such carpenters, such chips " (80d), " like to its like." " New. By the faith of my body, such carpenter, such chips, And as the wise man said, such lettuce, such lips. For, like master, like man : like tutor, like scholar ; And, like will to like, quoth the Devil to the Collier."—Fulwell, *Like Will to Like* (E.E.D.S.), 24d.

CART, (a) " set the cart before the horse " (79a), to begin at the wrong end ; to set things hind side before : Fr. " Il mettoyt la charette devant les beufz " (Rabelais). " He deemes that a preposterous govern-ment where the wife predominates, and the husband submits to her discretion, that is Hysterion and Proteron, the cart before the horse."—*Harry White, his Humour.*

(b) " the best cart may overthrow " (35a), " acci-dents may happen," " there's nothing certain save the unforeseen."

(c) " I am cast at cart's arse " (21b), in disgrace : offenders were formerly punished by being flogged when tied to the hinder part of a driven cart.

(d) " carts well driven go long upright " (35c), see section b supra.

CARVING, " he at meat carving her, and none else before, Now carved he to all but her, and her no more " (54b).

CASE, (a) " put case " (passim), to suppose or propose a hypothetical instance or illustration : an idiomatic expression formerly common in arguments. " Put case there be three brethren, John-a-Nokes, John-a-

Nash, and John-a-Stile."—*Returne from Parnassus* (1606).

(*b*) " clear out of the case " (32*a*), out of the running, beyond consideration.

CAST, " privy nips or casts overthwart the shins " (24*c*)—" even the like cast hast thou " (33*d*)—" ye neither care nor wellnigh cast what ye pay " (81*c*), both as subs. and verb *cast* was in full work—throw, motion, turn, glance, blow, advice, counsel, plan, design, object of desire, attempt at flight, skill, art, trick, juggle, fashion, form, pattern, shade, colour, tinge, chance, venture, touch, stroke, and many more glosses beside, each with their corresponding verbal usages.

CASTING, " far casting for commonwealth " (50*d*), roundabout search for joint benefit.

CAT, (*a*) " a cat may look on a king " (70*c*), a retort on impertinent or misplaced interference; there are certain things an inferior may do in the presence of a superior.

(*b*) " the cat would (or will) eat fish and would (or will) not wet her feet " (34*d*); cf. Shakspeare (*Macbeth*), " Letting, I dare not, wait upon, I would, Like the poor cat i' the adage." " Cat lufat visch, ac he nele his feth wete."—*MS. Trin. Coll. Camb.* (*c.* 1250).

(*c*) " a woman hath nine lives like a cat " (60*c*).

(*d*) " let the cat wink and let the mouse run " (61*b*).

(*e*) " it hath need be a wily mouse that should breed in the cat's ear " (71*d*). " A hardy mowse that is bold to breede In cattis eeris."—*Order of Foles,* MS. (*c.* 1450). " It is a wyly mouse That can build his dwellinge house Within the cattes eare."—Skelton (1520).

(*f*) " somewhat it is . . . when the cat winketh and both her eyne out " (61*a*).

(*g*) " cat after kind, good mouse hunt " (33*c*).

(*h*) " little and little the cat eateth the flickle " (82*b*).

(*i*) " no playing with a straw before an old cat " (88*a*).

(*j*) " the cat knoweth whose lips she licketh " (98*b*). " Li vilains reproche du chat Qu'il set bien qui barbes il leche."—*Des trois Dames qui trouvèrent un Anel* (*c.* 1300).

(*k*) " to turne the cat in the pan " (79*a*), to " rat " ; to reverse one's position through self-interest ; to play the turncoat ; the derivation is absolutely unknown ; *cat* =" cate " or " cake " is historically (says Murray) untenable. " Now am I true araid like a phesitien ; I am as very a turncote as the wethercoke of Poles ; For now I will calle my name Due Disporte. So, so, finely I can turne the catt in the pane."—*Wit and Wisdom* (E.E.D.S., *Anon. Pl.*, Ser. 4), 3 (*c.* 1559), " As for Bernard, often tyme he turneth the cat in the pan."—Shacklock, *Hatchet of Heresies* (1565).

(*l*) " my cat's leering look . . . showeth me that my cat goeth a catterwawing " (70*c*), *i.e.* is given to wantonness.

(*m*) " they two agreed like two cats in a gutter " (54*c*).

(*n*) " by scratching and biting cats and dogs come together " (54*c*).

(*o*) " when all candles be out cats be grey " (13*c*), cf. " If you cannot kiss the mistress kiss the maid " ; " Joan in the dark is as good as my lady."

CATCH, " catch that catch may " (*Epig.*), in modern form, " catch as catch can."

CAUSE, " cause causeth " (22*b*).

CHAIR, " every man may not sit in the chair " (46*c*), it is not given to everyone to rule ; all cannot be masters.

CHALK, " to compare in taste, chalk and cheese " (63*c*), to compare (or mistake) things utterly different. The modern form is " to know chalk from cheese "=to have one's wits about one, to know what is worthless from what is of value. " Lo ! how they feignen chalk for cheese."—Gower, *Confessio Amantis* (1393). " Though I have no learning, yet I know chese from chalke."—*John Bon and Mast Person* (1548). " Do not these thynges differ as muche as chalcke and chese? "—Shacklock, *Hatchet of Heresies* (1565). " To French and Scots so fayr a taell I tolde, That they beleeved whyt-chalk and chees was oen."—Churchyard, *Chippes* (1573).

(b) " alike in colour to deem ink and chalk " (63c), a variant of the foregoing entry.

CHANGE, " change be no robbery " (63b), an excuse for a forced or jesting imposition ; a delicate way of making a present : now usually " fair exchange is no robbery."

CHANGED, " would to God he and you had changed places " (80c).

CHAT, " no man may chat ought in ought of her charge " (24b), chat=talk. " Into a rapture lets her baby cry, While she chats him . . ."—Shakspeare, *Coriolanus* (1610), ii. 1.

CHATTING, " chatting to chiding is not worth a chute " (69a), it is hardly worth while to answer a scolding.

CHECK, " checks and choking oysters " (43c), taunts, reproaches : see Choking oyster.

CHECKER, " not checker a-board all was not clear in the coast " (89b). " Not as a checker, reprover, or despiser of other men's translations."—Coverdale, *Lewis's History of the Translations of the Bible into English, 95.*

CHEESE, " ye may see no green cheese, but your teeth must water " (97c), green cheese=cream cheese.

CHICKENS, (a) " there is a nest of chickens, which doth brood, That will sure make his hair grow through his hood " (66b), i.e. deceived, cuckolded as it were.

(b) " thy chickens tell aforehand " (*Epigrams*), reckon beforehand a successful issue.

CHIEVING (10d and 48d), doing, accomplishment.

CHILD, " burnt child, fire dreadeth " (55b), once bit, twice shy. " So that child withdraweth is hond, From the fur ant the brond, That hath byfore bue brend, Brend child fur dredth, Quoth Hendyng."—*Proverbs of Hendyng, MS. (c. 1320). " Timon.* Why urge yee me? my hart doth boyle with heate, And will not stoope to any of your lures : A burnt childe dreads the flyre."—*Timon (c.* 1590).

CHILDREN, (a) " children learn to creep ere they can go " (37b).

(b) " children and fools cannot lie " (38a). "Master Constable says : You know neighbours 'tis an old saw, Children and fools speake true."—Lyly, *Endimion* (1591).

(c) " better children weep than old men " (34b). It is related in connection with the Gowrie conspiracy, that King James VI., about to depart from Gowrie Castle, was forcibly prevented by the Master of Glammis, and as the tears started to the eyes of the young king, " better bairns weep than bearded men " was the other's observation.

(d) " ye have many godchildren to look upon, and ye bless them all, but ye bass but one " (84d).

CHIP, (a) " who lacketh a stock his gain is not worth a chip " (94c).

(b) " as merry as three chips " (17c), cf. Shakspeare's " dancing chips " (*Sonnets*, 128).

CHOKING OYSTERS, " checks and choking oysters " (43c), taunts and replies that put one to silence. " I have a stoppynge oyster in my poke."—Skelton, *Bowge of Court* (c. 1529), 477. " To a feloe laiyng to his rebuke that he was over deintie of his mouthe and diete, he did with this reason give a stopping oistre." —Udall, *Apoph.* (1542), 61.

CHURCH, " the nearer to the church, the further from God " (21a). " Qui est près de l'église est souvent loin de Dieu."—*Les Proverbes communs* (c. 1500).

CIRCUMQUAQUES (84d), far-fetched and roundabout stories.

CLARGY, " to put me to my clargy " (64b), see rhyme : *clergy*=learning, science, knowledge. " I rede how besy that he was Upon clergye, an hed of bras To forge and make it for to telle."—Gower, *MS. Soc. Antiq.*, 134, f. 104.

CLAW, (a) " thou makest me claw when it itcheth not " (85c).

(b) " claw a churl by th' arse and he shitteth in my hand " (80c).

CLAWED, " I clawed her by the back " (24d).

CLERKS, " the greatest clerks be not the wisest men "
(67a). " The greatest clerks ben not the wisest men,
As whilom to the wolf this spake the mare."—Chaucer,
Cant. Tales (1383), *Miller's Tale.* " Now I here wel, it
is treue that I long syth have redde and herde, that the
best clerkes ben not the wysest men."—*Historye of
Reynard the Foxe* (1481).

CLIMBED, " he that never climbed never fell " (46d).

CLOAK, " that cloak for the rain, soever ye bring me "
(69d). " *Nicholas.* 'Tis good to have a cloake for the
raine ; a bad shift is better then none at all ; Ile sit
heere, as if I were as dead as a doore naile."—*Two
Angry Women of Abingdon* (1599).

CLOCK, " and looked . . . what it was o'clock " (96b),
saw how matters stood ; became aware of the facts :
the phrase is still colloquial or slang. " To know
what ys a clocke."—Skelton, *Works* (c. 1513), ii. 132
(Dyce).

CLOG, " where nought is to wed with, wise men flee the
clog " (32a), originally *clog*=incumbrance ; hence a
wife : this definition occurs very early. " *Science.* Ye
have woon me for ever, dowghter, Although ye have
woon a clog wyth all. *Wyt.* A clogg, sweete hart,
what ? *Science.* Such as doth fall To all men that
joyne themselves in marriage."—*Wyt and Science* (c.
1540), *Anon. Plays*, 3 Ser. (E.E.D.S.). " The prince
himself is about a piece of iniquity, Stealing away
from his father with his clog at his heels."—Shakspeare, *Winter's Tale* (1604), iv. 4.

CLOTH, " it is a bad cloth that will take no colour " (92d).

CLOTHES, " to rent off my clothes from my back " (26b).

CLOUDS, " after clouds black we shall have weather
clear " (36c).

COAT, " cut my coat after my cloth " (20b), to adapt oneself to circumstances ; to measure expense by income.
A relic of the sumptuary laws : an early allusion occurs
in the interlude of *Godly Queene Hestor* (c. 1530) :
" There is a cause why, That I go not gay : I tell you of
a word, Aman that new lord, Hath brought up all
good clothe, And hath so many gowns, as would
serve ten towns, Be ye never so loth : And any man in

the town, do buy him a good gown, He is very wroth.
And will him straight tell, the statute of apparel Shall
teach him good " (E.E.D.S., *Anon Pl.*, 2nd Ser.).

COCK, " the young cock croweth as he the old heareth "
(23*c*), other readings are : " The young cock learneth
to crow of the old " (1509); " as the old cock crows so
does the chick " (1589).

(*b*) " every cock is proud on his own dunghill "
(31*b*), every man is a hero to his own circle ; each one
fights best with friends and backers about him.   " þet
fleshs is her et home, ase eorðe, þet is et eorðe : aut for
þui hit is cwointe˜t cwiuer, ᵉase mᵉ seið, þet coc is kene
on his owne mixenne."—þe *Ancren Riwle* (*c.* 1250).

COCKNEY, (*a*) " he that cometh every day shall have a
cockney, He that cometh now and then shall have a
fat hen " (44*a*). Murray breaks up M.E. *cokeney* into
coken ey=cock's egg, and defines the word when used
by Langland as " egg," a rendering which seems
confirmed in the present instance.   " I have no salt
bacon, Ne no cokeney, by Crist, coloppes for to make."
—Langland, *P. Plowman* (1363), 4370.

(*b*) " a good cockney coke " (97*d*), *i.e.* a cockney
cook : in derision and contempt, with perhaps a play
on *cokes*=fool.   The origin of *cockney* (=one born
within the sound of Bow Bells) has been much debated ;
but, says Dr. Murray, in the course of an exhaustive
statement (*Academy,* May 10, 1890, p. 320), " the history
of the word, so far as it means a person, is very clear
and simple.   We have the senses (1) ' cockered or pet
child,' ' nestle-cock,' ' mother's darling,' ' milksop,'
primarily the child, but continued to the squeamish
and effeminate man into which he grows up.   (2) A
nickname applied by country people to the inhabitants
of great towns, whom they considered ' milksops,' from
their daintier habits and incapacity for rough work.
York, London, Perugia, were, according to Harman,
all nests of cockneys.   (3) By about 1600 the name
began to be attached especially to Londoners, as the
representatives *par excellence* of the city milksop.
One understands the disgust with which a cavalier in
1641 wrote that he was ' obliged to quit Oxford at the
approach of Essex and Waller with their prodigious
number of cockneys.' "

COCKSCOMB, " to wear a cockscomb " (67d), the comb of a cock was one of the ensigns or tokens of a professional fool.

(c) " as oft change from hue to hue as doth the cocks of Ind " (31a), ? *Ind*=indigo, the allusion being to the changing sheen of the cock's bluish-black feathers.

(d) " he setteth cock on the hoop " (65d), gives way to reckless enjoyment; sets all by the ears; is proud, vaunting, and exultant.   " You'll make a mutiny among my guests! You will set cock-a-hoop! you'll be the man! "—Shakspeare, *Romeo and Juliet* (1595). i. 5.

COIN, " when coin is not common, commons must be scant " (51b).

COLD, " let them that be cold, blow at the coal " (29d). " Our talwod is all brent, Our faggottes are all spent, We may blow at the cole."—Skelton, *Why come ye not to Court* (c. 1520).

COLEPROPHET, " ye play coleprophet (quoth I) who taketh in hand To know his answer before he do his errand " (21a), *coleprophet*=a false prophet or cheat. " Coleprophet and cole-poyson, thou art both."—Heywood, *Ep.*, 89, *Cent.* vi.

COLL, " coll under canstick she can play in both hands " (24b), see Canstick. " Coll under canstyk she can plaie on both hands, Dissimulation well she understands " (see supra 24b).

COLLOP, " it is a dear collop that is cut out of th' own flesh " (28d). " God knows thou art a colup of my flesh."—Shakspeare, *1 Henry VI.* (1592), v. 5.

COLT, (a) " of a ragged colt there cometh a good horse " (33b). " *Touchstone*. This cannot be fained, sure. Heaven pardon my severitie! 'The ragged colt may prove a good horse.' "—Jonson, &c., *Eastward Hoe* (1605).

(b) " colts may prove well with tatches ill " (33b), *tache* (or *tatch*)=spot, blemish.

COME, (a) " come what, come would " (44b).
(b) " you come to your cost " (34a).

COMETH, " all cometh to one " (50*b*), in modern phrase, " all cometh to him that waits."

COMING, " it is ill coming to th' end of a shot and beginning of a fray " (79*c*).

COMMODITIES (10*b*), matters of advantage or convenience.

CONSITHER (5*b*), consider.

CONSTER (13*d*), construe, explain.

CONVEY (48*b*), steal. The classical quotation is of course from Shakspeare, and from the same authority I give illustrations of derivatives : the rendering was popular. " *Nym.* The good humour is, to steal at a minute's rest. *Pist.* Convey, the wise it call."— Shakspeare, *Merry Wives of Windsor* (1596), Act i., Sc. 3. " Since Henry's death, I fear there is conveyance."—Shakspeare, 1 *Henry VI.* (1592), i. 3. " O good convey ! Conveyers are you all, That rise thus nimbly by a true king's fall."—Shakspeare, *Richard II.* 1597), iv., *sub fin.*

COOK, " a poor cook that may not lick her own fingers " (89*b*). " He is an evyll coke y^t can not lycke his owne lippes."—*Vulgaria Stambrigi* (c. 1510). " *Capulet.* Sirrah, go hire me twenty cunning cooks. 2 *Servant.* You shall have none ill, sir ; for I'll try if they can lick their fingers."—Shakspeare, *Romeo and Juliet* (1595), iv. 2.

COOKQUEAN, see Cuckquean.

COPE, " segging is good cope " (94*a*), sedge is good covering.

CORD, " would to our lord ye had hanged both in one cord " (80*b*).

CORNER, " the corner of our case (quoth he) I you tell " (20*b*), *corner*=gist, the furthest point of probing.

CORSE, " my comely corse " (85*a*), body.

COST, " all was not clear in the cost " (89*b*), *i.e.* coast.

COUCH, " couch a hogshead " (58*b*), go to sleep : *hogshead*=head. " I couched a hogshead in a skypper this darkmans."—Harman, *Caveat* (1567), 66 (1814).

COUGH, " thou canst cough in the aumbry " (82d),
aumbry=cupboard, pantry. " Some slovens from
sleeping no sooner be up, But hand is in aumbrie, and
nose in the cup."—Tusser, *Five Hundred Points*
(1573), ii. 5.

COUNTERPOISE, " whether they counterpaise or out-
weigh " (10a), counterpoise.

COURT, " I was neither of court nor of counsel made "
(43b), *i.e.* neither approached for advice, nor invited
to express an opinion.

COVET, " all covet, all lose " (97c).

COVETISE (12c), covetousness.

COW, (a) " the cow is wood " (78d), *wood*=mad, furious.
    (b) " God sendeth the shrewd cow short horns "
(27c), *shrewd*=malicious, badly disposed. " The Bishop of Sarum sayd, That he trusted ere Christmas
Day to visit and cleanse a good part of the kingdom.
But most commonly God sendeth a shrewd cow short
horns, or else many a thousand in England had
smarted."—Foxe, *Acts and Manuments.*
    (c) " as comely as a cow in a cage " (52d).
    (d) " Margery, good cow, gave a good meal, but
then she cast it down again with her heel " (86a).
    (e) " every man as he loveth, Quoth the good man,
when that he kissed his cow " (53a).
    (f) " many a good cow hath an evil calf " (28a).

COW-CALF, " as well for the cow-calf as for the bull "
(62a).

COY, " as coy as a croker's mare " (52b), *croker*=
saffron-dealer.

CRABS, " the greatest crabs be not all the best meat "
(40d).

CRIPPLE, " it is hard halting before a cripple " (71d).
" I perceyve (quod she) it is evill to halte before a
creple . . . and it is evill to hop before them that
runne for the bell."—Gascoigne, *Fable of Ferdinando
Jeronimi and Leonora de Valases* (1575).

CROSS, (a) " now will I make a cross on this gate " (43d),
the cross as the emblem of disappointment and mis-
fortune ; and the fact that many pieces of money were

stamped on one side with a cross gave rise to many quibbles : see Cross *b* and *c* infra, and cf. Heywood, *Epigrams* (E.E.D.S., *Works*, ii. 226*b*), " I will make a cross upon his gate ; yea, cross on, Thy crosses be on gates all, in thy purse none."

(*b*) " I cross thee quite out of my book " (44*a*).

(*c*) " since thou art cross failed, avail, unhappy hook " (44*a*), *cross*=money (see *a* supra) ; *unhappy hook*=a commiserating address. " Now I have never a crose to blesse me, Now I goe a-mumming, Like a poore pennilesse spirit, Without pipe or druming."— *Marriage of Witt and Wisdome,* 1579 (E.E.D.S., *Anon. Plays,* Ser. 4). " Not a penny, not a penny ; you are too impatient to bear crosses."—Shakspeare, 2 *Henry IV.* (1598), i. 2.

CROW, (*a*) " we have a crow to pull " (70*d*), complaint to make, quarrel, a bone to pick. " *Abelle.* Dere brother, I will fayre On feld ther our bestes ar, To looke if they be holgh or fulle. *Cayn.* Na, na, abide, we have a craw to pulle."—Mactacio Abel, in *Towne-ley Mysteries* (c. 1420).

(*b*) " the crow thinketh his own birds fairest in the wood " (61*c*). " It must needs be good ground that brings forth such good corne ; When I look on him, methinks him to be evill favoured, Yet the crowe thinkes her black birds of all other the fairest."— Lupton, *All for Money* (1578).

(*c*) " as good to say, the crow is white " (69*a*), *i.e.* " You're talking nonsense, or worse, telling lies."

CRUMMETH, " cracketh and crummeth " (79*a*), crumbleth.

CRY A LEISON (78*b*), *i.e.* Kyrie eleison (" Lord, have mercy "), a short petition used at the beginning of the Roman Mass. The phrase was early the subject of punning allusions. Tyndale uses it in the sense of a complaint or scolding (*Obed. Chr. Man,* 130*b*, 1528) ; and Heywood, in the present instance, appar-ently means something of the same kind, with an added sarcasm in his corrupted orthography, " cry a leison " (= a cry *à* [*la*] Alison, which appears (89*b*) to be the name of the wife of whom the husband is speaking).

CUCKQUEAN, " ye make her a cookquean " (76*b*), a female cuckold : here possibly also a play on " cook."

HEY. PROV.   K

CUNNING, " that cunning man " (66d), orig. knowledge, skill, learning, no bad sense being implied : as early as the time of Lord Bacon, however, the word was on the down-grade in meaning, influenced, no doubt, by the mundane truth that skill in the hands of the unscrupulous is used to defraud those less gifted. " If I forget thee, O Jerusalem, let my right hand forget her cunning."—*Bible*, Auth. Vers. (1611), *Psalm* cxxxvii. 5. " With all the cunning manner of our flight, Determined of."—Shakspeare, *Two Gent.*, ii. 4.

CUPSHOTTEN, " somewhat cupshotten " (31a), drunk.

CURRYFAVEL, " they can curryfavel and make fair weather " (66b), *curryfavel*=flatter.

CUSHION, (a) " ye missed the cushion, for all your haste " (97c), idiomatic : from the practice of archery =to fail in an attempt, to miss the point. " Trulie, Euphues, you have mist the cushion, for I was neither angrie with your long absence, neither am I well pleased at your presence."—Lyly, *Euphues* (1581).
(b) " I may set you beside the cushion " (97c), *i.e.* pass over with contempt, ignore, shelve. " Thus is he set beside the cushion, for his sincerity and forwardness in the good cause."—Spalding, i. 291.

DAGGER, (a) " he beareth a dagger in his sleeve " (35b), *i.e.* hidden, in reserve, ready for use.
(b) " it be ill playing with short daggers " (47c), in modern phrase, " edged tools."

DAIMENT, " sufferancee is no quittance in this daiment " (64d), ? judgment, settlement : cf. *daysman*=umpire, arbitrator. *Day* (in legal sense)=return of a writ, appearance.

DAME, " he that will not be ruled by his own dame shall be ruled by his stepdame " (92d).

DANCE, " sufferance is your dance " (68b), rôle, lot : cf. " to lead one a dance."

DANCETH, " he danceth attendance " (*Epigrams*), to wait upon constantly and obsequiously.

DARLING, " it is better to be an old man's darling than a young man's warling " (80a), *warling* is of doubtful origin, occurring only in this proverb ; perhaps coined from war, in imitation of darling, and meaning one often quarrelled with.

DAW (*passim*), an empty-headed, foolish fellow. " He that for commyn welth bysyly Studyeth and laboryth, and lyveth by Goddes law, Except he waxe ryche, men count hym but a daw ! "—*Four Elements* (*c.* 1510), *Anon. Plays,* Ser. 1 (E.E.D.S.), 4*d.* " Good faith, I am no wiser than a daw."—Shakspeare, 1 *Henry VI.* (1592), ii. 4.

DAY, (*a*) " one day was three till liberty was borrow " (27*c*), *borrow*=pledged, mortgaged.

(*b*) " I see day at this little hole " (26*b*), in modern phrase, " daylight "; an echo, possibly, of another proverbial saying—" It is always darkest before the dawn."

(*c*) " I will say no more till the day be longer " (*Epigrams*).

(*d*) " be the day never so long, evermore at last they ring to evensong " (82*b*). " For though the day be never so long At last the bell rings for evensong."—Hawes, *Pastime of Pleasure.*

(*e*) " the day of doom shall be done " (85*a*).

(*f*) " farewell, my good days, they will be soon gone " (57*a*).

DEAD, (*a*) " for gain (he) is dead and laid in tomb " (66*a*).

(*b*) " I have . . . a dead man's head in my dish " (80*b*), the " dear departed " of modern phrase. " As bold-fac'd women, when they wed another, Banquet their husbands with their dead love's heads."—Marston, *Insatiate Countess.*

DEAF, (*a*) " then were ye deaf, ye could not hear on that side " (90*d*), *i.e.* wilfully deaf.

(*b*) " who is so deaf as he that will not hear? " (*Epigrams*).

DEAR, (*a*) " whoso that knew what would be dear, should need be a marchant but one year " (4*b*).

(*b*) " dear bought and far fet are dainties for ladies " (38*d*), *fet*=fetched. " Some far fet trick, trick good for ladies, some stale toy or other."—Marston, *Malcontent* (1604). " *Niece.* Ay, marry, sir, this was a rich conceit indeed. *Pompey.* And far fetched; therefore good for you, lady.''—Beaumont and Fletcher, *Wit at Several Weapons* (1614).

DEAREST, "to buy the dearest for the best alway" (81c), cf. "cheap and nasty."

DEATH, (a) " death ! . . . . take me that time, to take a breath " (45a), waiting for dead men's shoes profiteth little.

(b) "though love decree departure death to be" (48d).

DEED, "deed without words" (71b).

DESERT, "desert and reward be ofttimes things far odd " (42a).

DEVIL, (a) "the devil hath cast a bone to set strife " (57c).

(b) "young saint, old devil " (27c), this occurs in *MS. Harleian* (c. 1490).

(c) "he must have a long spoon that would sup (or eat) with the devil " (71d). "Therefore behoveth him a ful long spone, That shal ete with a fend : thus herd I say."—Chaucer, *Squieres Tale* (*Cant. Tales, c.* 1383). " *Courtesan.* Will you go with me? *Dromio.* Master, if you do, expect spoonmeat or bespeak a long spoon. *Antipholus.* Why, Dromio? *Dromio.* Marry, he must have a long spoon that must eat with the devil."—Shakspeare, *Comedy of Errors* (1593), iv. 3.

(d) "like as the devil looked over Lincoln " (91c). "The middle or Rood tower of Lincoln Cathedral is the highest in the whole kingdom, and when the spire was standing on it, it must, in proportion to the height of the tower, have exceeded that of old St. Paul's, which was five hundred and twenty feet. The monks were so proud of this structure, that they would have it that the devil looked upon it with an envious eye : whence the proverb of a man who looks invidious and malignant, ' he looks as the devil over Lincoln.' "—*Tour through England and Wales* (1742). Ray gives another account : " It is probable that it took its rise from a small image of the devil standing on the top of Lincoln College, in Oxford."—*Proverbs* (1737).

(e) "he must needs go when the devil doth drive " (78c). " There is a proverb which trewe now preveth,

He must nedes go that the dyvell dryveth."—Heywood, *Johan Johan, Tyb, and Syr Jhan.*

(*f*) " the devil is no falser than, he " (71*d*).

(*g*) " the devil go with thee, down the lane " (83*d*).

(*h*) " meet to set the devil on sale " (77*b*).

(*i*) " the devil in th' orloge " (63*d*). " Some for a tryfull pley the devyll in the orloge."—Harman, *Vulgaria* (1530).

(*j*) " the devil is dead " (91*c*).

(*k*) " the devil with his dam hath more rest in hell than I with thee " (85*b*).

(*l*) " the devil's good grace might have given a greeting " (99*c*).

(*m*) " I will not bear the devil's sack " (73*d*), compound a wrong.

(*n*) " what change may compare to the devil's life like his that has chosen a devil to his wife? " (74*c*).

DIEU-GARD, " a beck as good as a dieu-gard " (29*d*), a salutation, " God save you ! " " Each beck of yours shall be in stead of a diew garde unto me."—Florio, *Second Frutes* (1591), 81.

DINNERS, " dinners cannot be long, where dainties want " (51*b*).

DISCRIVE (16*a*), describe.

DISEASED, " more diseased by early lying down " (55*c*), *disease* formerly was generic for " absence of ease."

DISH, (*a*) " I may break a dish there " (38*d*), have a meal, take pot-luck, ply knife and fork.

(*b*) " as well as the beggar knoweth his dish (or bag)," see Bag.

DO, " it is as folk do and not as folk say " (73*b*).

DONE, (*a*) " as good undone as do it too soon " (74*a*).

(*b*) " things done cannot be undone " (26*a*).

(*c*) " better it be done than wish it had been done " (74*a*).

DOCK, " in dock, out nettle " (54*d*), a charm for a nettle sting which early passed into a proverb expressive of inconstancy. " Ye wete well Ladie eke (quoth I) that I have not plaid racket, Nettle in, Docke out, and with this the weathercocke waved."—

Chaucer, *Testament of Love.* " Is this my in dock, out nettle? "—Middleton, *More Dissemblers besides Women* (1623).

DOE, " when he hunteth a doe that he cannot avow all dogs bark not at him " (72*a*).

DOG, (*a*) " a man may handle his dog so that he may make him bite him " (85*c*).

(*b*) " when he hunteth a doe that he cannot avow all dogs bark not at him " (72*a*).

(*c*) " it is a poor dog that is not worth the whistling " (43*b*).

(*d*) " unable to give a dog a loaf " (81*b*).

(*e*) " a dog will bark ere he bite " (85*b*).

(*f*) " she will lie as fast as a dog will lick a dish " (78*a*).

(*g*) " a dog hath a day " (36*d*), or, in modern phrase, " every dog has its day "; *i.e.* a period during which he is in his prime.

(*h*) " an old dog biteth sore " (75*b*). " Olde dogges bite sore."—Churchyard, *Handeful of Gladsome Verses* (1592).

(*i*) " it is hard to make an old dog stoop " (85*c*).

(*j*) " to help a dog over a stile " (39*b*), the modern version has " lame dog ": to give a hand, to assist in difficulty. " Here is a stile so high as a man cannot help a dog over it."—Marston, *Insatiate Countess* (1605), ii. 2.

(*k*) " a hair of the dog that bit us last night " (45*c*), a pick-me-up after a debauch : apparently a memory of the superstition, which was and still is common, that, being bitten by a dog, one cannot do better than pluck a handful of hair from him, and lay it on the wound. Old receipt books advise that an inebriate should drink sparingly in the morning some of the same liquor which he had drunk to excess overnight.

(*l*) " it is ill waking of a sleeping dog " (30*a*), cf. " let sleeping dogs lie."

(*m*) " at every dog's bark, seem not to awake " (68*d*).

(*n*) " hungry dogs will eat dirty puddings " (14*a*), another proverb declares that a hungry man will eat anything, except Suffolk cheese.

DOLE, (a) "his dole is soon done" (37d), lot, share. *Happy man be your dole* = a general wish for success. "Happy man be his dole that misses her."—*Grim the Collier of Croydon.*

(b) "ye deal this dole out of a wrong door" (9d), your charity is ill bestowed.

DOON (30c), done.

DOOR, (a) "it is good to have a hatch before the door" (32c), *hatch* = a wooden partition coming over the lower half of a doorway and leaving open the upper half.

(b) see Dole.

(c) "he turned her out of doors to graze on the plain" (99d).

DOTING, "after a doting and drunken deed, let submission obtain some mercy or meed" (28c), *doting* = foolish, silly.

DOYT (80c), doth.

DRAFF, "the still sow eats up all the draf" (27c)— "draf is your errand, but drink ye would" (31d), *draff* = dregs, dirt, refuse, anything thrown away as unfit for food. " 'Tis old but true, Still swine eat all the draff."—Shakspeare, *Merry Wives* (1596), iv. 2.

DRAWLATCH, see John Drawlatch.

DREDE (75b), fear: in a lesser degree than is usually conveyed by the word.

DRINK, (a) "I drink (quoth she); quoth he, I will not pledge" (60d).

(b) see Draff.

DRUNK, (a) "drunk in the good ale glass" (45c), *i.e.* in a state of "alecie."

(b) "he that killeth a man when he is drunk shall be hanged when he is sober" (28c).

DRIVEL, "drivel and drudge" (83b), *drivel* = servant. "To encourage the husband to use his wife as a vile dreuell."—Udall, *Corinth.*, ch. xi.

DUCK, "like a duke? like a duck!" (86b), a play on words.

DUNSTABLE, " as plain as Dunstable highway " (69b),
plain Dunstable=anything homely, plain, simple—
why, is not clear : sometimes *byeway*. " These men
walked by-wayes, and the saying is, many by-walkers,
many balkes, many balkes, much stumbling, and
where much stumbling is, there is sometime a fall ;
howbeit there were some good walkers among them,
that walked in the king's high way ordinarily, upright, plaine Dunstable way."—Latimer, *Sermons*
(*d.* 1555).

DUR (9d, 20c, 26b, 32c, &c.), door (A.S.).

DYKE, " my beautiful marriage lieth in the dyke " (8b).

EAR, (a) " in at the one ear and out of the t'other "
(92d). " But Troilus, that nigh for sorrow deide,
Tooke little hede of all that ever he ment ; One eare
it heard, at the other out it went."—Chaucer, *Troilus
and Creseide* (1369).
    (b) " her ears might well glow, for all the town
talked of her " (52c), that the ears burn when talked
of by someone absent is still a prevalent superstition.
    (c) " you had on your harvest ears, thick of hear-
ing " (91a). " Thine eares be on pilgrimage, or in
the wildernes, as they say commonly, thou hast on
thy harvest eares, *vestræ peregrinantur aures.*"—
Withal, *Dictionary* (1608), 46.
    (d) " he must both tell you a tale and find you ears "
(91a).
    (e) " by the ears " (54d), quarrelling, at strife.
" Were half to half the world by the ears, and he
Upon my party, I'd revolt."—Shakspeare, *Coriolanus*
(1610), i. 1.

EARLY " early up and never the near " (6d), *near*=
nearer. " Better far off, than near be ne'er the
near."—Shakspeare, *Richard II.* (1597), v. 1.

EAST, " the longer east, the shorter west " (50b).

EBB, (a) " he was at an ebb, though he be now afloat "
(38b), in difficulties or hard up, but now in better
circumstances.
    (b) " thou art at an ebb in Newgate " (*Epigrams*).

EEL, " as sure to hold as an eel by the tail " (24*c*), *i.e.*
slippery, unreliable. " Cauda tenes anguillam : you
have an eele by the taile."—Withal, *Dictionary* (ed.
1634), 554. " Paulo momento huc illuc impellitur.
Hee is as wavering as a wethercocke. He is heere
and their all in a moment. Theirs as much holde to
his word, as to take a wet eele by the taile."—
Terence in English (1614).

EEL-SKINS, " we shall see him prove a merchant of eel-
skins " (66*c*).

EGGS, " in came the third, with his V eggs " (52*c*),
see Heywood, *Works* (E.E.D.S.), II. 220*b*.

END, (*a*) " some loose or odd end will come . . . some
. . . day " (45*a*).
  (*b*) " such beginning, such end " (94*b*).
  (*c*) " the game from beginning sheweth what end is
meant " (75*d*).

ENOUGH, (*a*) " enough is enough " (103*a*). " And of
enough enough, and nowe no more, Bycause my
braynes no better can devise . . . . It is enough and as
good as a feast."—Gascoigne, *Memories* (1575).
  (*b*) " enough is as good as a feast " (103*a*). " It
is an olde proverb He is well at ese y^t hath enough
and can say ho. He hath enough, holy doctours say,
to whom his temporall godes be they never so fewe
suffisen to him and to his, to fynde them that them
nedyth."—*Dives and Pauper* (1493).
  (*c*) " he that knoweth when he hath enough is no
fool " (81*c*).
  (*d*) " here is enough and too much " (82*c*).

ENVIED, " better be envied than pitied " (32*a*).

ERRAND, (*a*) " thus is thine errand sped " (79*d*).
  (*b*) " I am sped of mine errand " (101*c*).

EVEN, " I shall be even with him " (31*c*), on equality
with, quits with : now chiefly colloquial.

EVERYCHONE (5*d*), everyone.

EXTREMITIES, " flee th'attempting of extremities " (68*c*),
i.e. avoid the harshest measures.

EYE, (*a*) " I might put my winning in mine eye and
see never the worse " (42*a*). " You have had con-

ferences and conferences again at Poissy and other
places, and gained by them just as much as you
might put in your eye, and see never the worse."—
Bramhall, *Works*, i. 68. " Bating Namure, he might
have put all the glorious harvests he yearly reap'd
there into his eye, and not have prejudic'd his royal
sight in the least."—T. Brown, *Works* (d. 1682),
ii. 329.

(*b*) " better eye out than alway ache " (19*d*).

(*c*) " he winketh with the one eye and looketh out
of the other " (40*b*).

(*d*) " that the eye seeth not, the heart reweth not "
78*c*). " The blinde eats many a flie, and much water
runnes by the mill that the miller never knowes of :
the evill that the eye sees not, the hart rues not."—
Greene, *Never too Late* (1590).

(*e*) " blame me not to haste for fear mine eye be
bleared " (8*d*), *haste* = hastily.

EYESORE, " it is but an eye sore " (13*b*). " Quod the
Barbour, but a lytell eye sore."—*Merry Jests of the
Wyddow Edyth* (1525).

FABLING, " without fabling " (15*b*), exaggerate, draw
the long bow, lie. " Without fable or guile."—*Four
Elements* (*c.* 1500), E.E.D.S., *Anon Plays*, Ser. 1.

FACE, (*a*) " I did set a good face on the matter "
(*Epigrams*), make the best of things.

(*b*) " two faces in one hood " (23*d*), double-dealing,
shuffling, two-faced. " *Alberto.* Not play two parts
in one? away, away, 'tis common fashion. Nay, if
you cannot bear two subtle fronts under one hood ;
ideot, goe by, goe by ; off this world's stage ! O
times impuritie ! "—*Antonio and Mellida* (1602).

(*c*) " their faces told toys " (17*d*), told tales : see
Toys.

FAIR, (*a*) " the fair lasteth all the year " (57*b*), *i.e.*
any time or every day is meet for the purpose : see
next entry.

(*b*) " a day after the fair " (20*a*), too late, when
everything is over.

(*c*) " fair words did fet " (53*c*), politeness costs
nothing *fet* = fetch.

(d) "the grace of God is worth a fair " (46d), a matter or affair to remember.

(e) "the fair and the foul by dark are like store " (13c), comparisons are not always possible ; under some circumstances quality is no matter ; in the dark all cats are grey.

FAIR AND WELL (96d), farewell.

FALL, "to fall in and not to fall out " (31a), to concur and agree, and not to disagree, quarrel, or fall at odds with.

FALSE, (a) "I fear false measures " (73d).
  (b) "as false as fair " (94c).
  (c) "as false as God is true " (78a).

FALSEHOOD, "falsehood in fellowship " (69c), *fellowship* =companionship : in the *Epigrams* occurs "there is falsehood in fellowship."

FANCY, "fancy may bolt bran and make ye take it flour " (62c), make-believe counts for much.

FAR, (a) "I have seen as far come as nigh " (34a), the drip of water wears away the stone.
  (b) "things erst so far off, were now so far on " (96d).

FARE, (a) "ye see your fare, set your heart at rest " (43d).
  (b) "fare ye well how ever I fare " (43d).

FAREN, "have gone further and have faren worse " (62c), *faren*=fared. "How has thou faren in far land ? "—*Towneley Mysteries*, 48.

FAREWELL, "farewell and feed full—that love ye well to do, but you lust not to do that longeth thereto " (34c), *i.e.* like to live well without the right to do so.

FART, (a) "I shall get a fart of a dead man as soon as a farthing " (37d).
  (b) "they that will be afraid of every fart must go far to piss " (69c).

FARTHING, (a) "she thinketh her farthing good silver " (26d). "Take example at me ; I tell you I thought my halfpeny good silver within these few yeares past, and no man esteemeth me unlesse it be for counsell."
—Gascoigne, *Glasse of Government* (1575).

(b) " but for a farthing who ever did sell you might boast you to be better sold than bought " (27a).

(c) " one farthing worth of good " (26b), a low standard of value.

FASHION, " every man after his fashion " (38c), probably a pun (a common one at the time) on *fashion* = farcy. " *Sh.* What shall we learn by travel? *An.* Fashions. *Sh.* That's a beastly disease."—*Old Fortunatus* (1600).

FAST, " fast bind, fast find " (8d). " Wherefore a plaine bargain is best, and in bargaines making; fast bind, fast find."—*Jests of Scogin* (1565). " Do, as I bid you, Shut doors after you; Fast bind, fast find; A proverb never stale in thrifty mind."—Shakspeare, *Merchant of Venice* (1598), ii. 5.

FAT, (a) " the fat is in the fire " (8b), all is confusion, all has failed: of failures and the results of sudden and unexpected revelations and disappointments. " Faith, Doricus, thy braine boils; keele it, keele it, or all the fatt's in the fire."—Marston, *What You Will* (1607).

(b) " a swine over-fat is cause of his own bane " (81d).

(c) " little knoweth the fat sow what the lean doth mean " (30a).

(d) " the fat clean flit from my beard " (9a).

FAULT, (a) " he hath but one fault, he is nought " (35c).

(b) " hard is for any man all faults to mend " (35c).

FAULTLESS, " he is lifeless that is faultless " (35c), *i.e.* perfection is not attained during life.

FAVER (5a), favour: see the rhyme " have her " in next line.

FEATHER, (a) " she may not bear a feather but she must breathe " (26d), *i.e.* much ado about nothing, mountains made of molehills.

(b) " if your meet-mate and you meet together, then shall we see two men bear a feather " (42c), of means employed altogether disproportionate to the end in view.

(c) " I got not so much . . . as a good hen's feather or a poor eggshell " (44b), said of altogether inadequate results.

(d) " he would fain flee, but he wanteth feathers " (35c), condition, substance : compare the modern " not a feather to fly with."

FED, (a) " better fed than taught " (25b).

(b) " he that gapeth till he be fed may fortune to fast and famish far longer " (21c), " if you want a thing done, do it yourself," " God helps those who help themselves," " he that will not work cannot eat."

FEED, " feed by measure and defy the physician " (81d), *i.e.* use and not abuse things ; temperance bringeth health.

FEET, (a) " he thinketh his feet be where his head shall never come " (35c).

(b) " here is since thou camest too many feet abed " (79d), *i.e.* you are not wanted, are *de trop*; your room is desired more than your company.

FERNE, " old ferne years " (5d), long ago, bygone. " Farewel al the snowgh of ferne yere."—Chaucer, *Troilus and Creseide* (1369), v. 1176.

FERRE, " as far as matter . . . served " (89d), far.

FET, " fet him in some stay " (32a)—" ye can fet as much " (95c), fetch. " From thence we fet a compass."—*Bible*, Author. Ver. (1611), *Acts* xxviii. 13. [Such archaisms in the Scriptures were not completely changed until well into the eighteenth century.]

FETTERS, (a) " no man loveth his fetters be they made of gold " (19c). " Who would weare fetters though they were all of gold? Or to be sicke, though his faint browes, for wearing night-cap, wore a crown."—Webster, *Sir T. Wyatt* (1607).

(b) " were I loose from the lovely links of my chain I would not dance in such fair fetters again " (19c).

FEW, " few know and fewer care " (100b).

FEWER, " the fewer, the better fare " (79c).

FIELDS, (a) " fields have eyes and woods have ears "
(70b), now usually " walls have ears." " The were
bettur be still; Wode has erys felde has siȝt Were
the forster here now right, Thy wordis shuld like the
ille."—*King Edward and the Shepherd*, MS. (c. 1300).
(b) " bidding me welcome strangely over the fields "
(40d).

FILTH, " a false flattering filth " (23d), a generic term
of contempt—slut, slattern, or worse. " If the filth
be in doubt."—*Gammer Gurton's Needle* (c. 1562),
E.E.D.S., *Anon. Plays, Ser. 3, 136d.*

FIND, " ye seek to find things ere they be lost " (34a),
i.e. you are " too previous."

FINDETH, " he findeth that seeks " (25b).

FINE, " in fine " (45d), in conclusion, finally, to sum up.
" In fine, delivers me to fill the time, Herself most
chastely absent."—Shakspeare, *All's Well that Ends
Well* (1598), iii. 7.

FINGER, (a) " [folly] to put my finger too far in the fire "
(57d), *i.e.* to meddle or interfere too much.
(b) " to make me put my finger in a hole " (73c).
(c) " with a wet finger ye can fet as much as
may easily all this matter ease " (95c), *i.e.* easily,
readily : as easy as turning over the leaf of a book,
or rubbing out writing on a slate. " He darting an
eye upon them, able to confound a thousand conjurers
in their own circles, though with a wet finger they
could fetch up a little divell."—Dekker, *A Strange
Horse-Race* (1613), sig. D 3.
(d) " each finger is a thumb " (66a), of clumsy
handling. " Each finger is a thumb to-day, methinks."
—Udall, *Roister Doister* (1534), i. 3. (E.E.D.S.,
Works, 20d).
(e) " I suck not this out of my own finger's end "
(43a).
(f) " I perfectly feel even at my finger's end "
(14c), *i.e.* know perfectly, am fully familiar with.

FIRE, (a) " where fire is, smoke will appear " (70a), there
is no effect without a cause : see *infra.*
(b) " there is no fire without some smoke " (69d),
see *supra.*

(c) " make no fire, raise no smoke " (60d), see *supra*.

(d) " soft fire maketh sweet malt " (6c), gentle means are best; take things quietly. " O Maister Philip, forbeare; you must not leape over the stile before you come at it; haste makes waste; soft fire makes sweet malt; not too far for falling; there's no hast to hang true men."—Haughton, *Two Angry Women of Abington* (1599).

(e) " fire in the one hand and water in the other " (24a).

(f) " to lay fire and tow together " (73c), to court danger or disaster.

FISH, (a) " fish is cast away that is cast in dry pools " (34c).

(b) " she is neither fish nor flesh nor good red herring " (24d), nondescript; neither one thing nor another; neither hay nor grass. " Wone that is nether flesshe nor fisshe."—Roy, *Rede me and be nott Wrothe* (1528), i. iij. b. " *Prince Henry.* An otter, sir John ! why an otter? *Falstaff.* Why? she is neither fish nor flesh; a man knows not where to have her."—Shakspeare, 2 *Henry IV.* (1598), iv. 3.

(c) " old fish and young flesh doth men best feed " (61d), *i.e.* mature fish and young womanhood.

(d) " all is fish that cometh to net " (30c), all serves the purpose. " But now (aye me) the glasing christal glasse Doth make us thinke that realmes and townes are rych, Where favour sways the sentence of the law, Where al is fishe that cometh to net."—Gascoigne, *Steele Glas* (1575).

FISHED, " he hath well fished and caught a frog " (32a). " Well I have fished and caught a frog, Brought little to pass with much ado."—Latimer, *Remains.*

FISHING, " it is ill fishing before the net " (38d).

FIT, (a) " by that surfeit . . . I feel a little fit " (55c), disorder, out of sorts.

(b) " for beginning this was a feat fit " (57c), contest, struggle, fight.

FLEA, " a flea in his ear " (35a), an annoying suggestion or experience, a good scolding.

FLEABITING, " but a fleabiting " (57c), a trifle, anything of little or no moment. " Their miseries are but flea-bitings to thine."—Burton, *Anat. Melan.* (1621).

FLEBERGEBET (25b), here=sycophant, smooth-tongued talker. " And when these flatterers and flibbergibbes another day shall come and claw you by the back, your grace may answer them thus."—Latimer, *Sermons* (d. 1555), fol. 39.

FLEE, " flee charge and find ease " (34c), *charge*=business, matters, affairs, anxieties, cares, responsibility.

FLEK, " flek and his make " (70a), *flek*=a generic reproach (of man or woman), specifically in contempt as of something altogether insignificant ; *make*=companion. " Fie upon me ! 'tis well known I am the mother Of children, scurvy fleak ! 'tis not for nought You boil eggs in your gruel."—Davenant, *The Wits* (1636).

FLESH, " it will not out of the flesh that is bred in the bone " (87c), *i.e.* cannot be eradicated ; in modern phrase, " What's bred in the bone will come out in the flesh." " He values me at a crack'd three farthings, for aught I see. It will never out of the flesh that's bred in the bone. I have told him enough, one would think, if that would serve ; but counsel to him is as good as a shoulder of mutton to a sick horse."—Jonson, *Every Man in his Humour* (1596).

FLETCHER, " mend as the fletcher mends his bolt " (91a), *i.e.* not at all. " Her mind runs sure upon a fletcher, or a bowyer ; however, I'll inform against both ; the fletcher for taking whole money for pieced arrows ; the bowyer for horning the headmen of his parish, and taking money for his pains."—Rowley, *Match at Midn.*, O. Pl. (Reed), vii. 378.

FLIES, " hungry flies bite sore " (91c).

FLIM-FLAM (24b), a lie, imposition.

FLINGING, " by flinging from your folks at home " (91b), *flinging*=departing hastily, " rushing off."

FLOWER, " she is not only the fairest flower in your garland, but also she is all the fair flower thereof " (88b).

FOAL, " how can the foal amble if the horse and mare trot? " (33c).

FOLLOW, " the wise man at all times to follow can find " (82a).

FOND, " to wed with me fond are " (4d), *fond*=pleased, delighted, eager.

FOOL, (a) " There is no fool to the old fool " (56b). " Comedie upon comedie he shall have; a morall, a historie, a tragedie, or what he will. One shal be called *the Doctor's dumpe* . . . and last *a pleasant Enterlude of No Foole to the Olde Foole*, with a jigge at the latter end in English hexameters of *O Neighbour Gabriel!! and his wooing of Kate Cotton.*"—Nash, *Have with you to Saffron Walden* (1596).

   (b) " a fool's bolt soon shot " (58d), in quotation *sot*=fool. " Sot is sot, and that is sene; For he wel speke wordes grene, Er ther hue buen rype. ' Sottes bolt is sone shote,' Quoth Hendyng."—*Proverbs of Hendyng*, MS. (c. 1320).

   (c) " fair words make fools fain " .(69b). " When thou art become one of that courtlie trayne, Thinke on this proverbe olde, quod he, that faire woordes make fools faine."—*Paradyse of Dayntie Devises* (1578).

   (d) " God sendeth fortune to fools " (75d); cf. " God watches over children, drunkards, and fools."

FOOT, (a) " he loveth her better at the sole of the foot than ever he loved me at the heart root " (70d).

   (b) " wrap it in the clothes and tread it under foot " (63d).

   (c) " folk shew much folly, when things should be sped, to run to the foot, that may go to the head " (67b). " Thou that stondys so sure on sete, Ware lest thy hede falle to thy fete."—*The Boke of Curtasye*, MS. (c. 1350).

FORGAVE, " he forgave her, as he forgiven would be " (90a).

FORGIVE, " to forgive and forget " (90a).

FORGIVEN, " forgiven and forgotten " (59b).

FORSPEAK, " forspeak not your future " (38c), gainsay.

FOSTER, " no longer foster, no longer lemman " (96c), *foster*=to cherish, indulge, harbour ; *lemman*= darling, beloved one.

FOUGHTEN, " a hard foughten field where no man escaped unkilled " (45d).

FOUL, (a) " foul water as soon as fair will quench hot fire " (13c).
   (b) " though her mouth be foul she hath a fair tail " (13d), *i.e.* though she be shrewish yet her person is desirable.

FOX, (a) " be a man never so greedy to win, He can have no more of the fox than the skin " (96a).
   (b) " when the fox preacheth, then beware your geese " (82c).

'FRAID, " more 'fraid than hurt " (11c).

FRIDAY, " he may his part on Good Friday eat and fast never the worse " (36a), *i.e.* have nothing, Good Friday being a " black " or total fast.

FRIEND, (a) " a friend is never known till a man hath need " (46a).
   (b) " prove thy friend ere thou have need " (46a).
   (c) " ye may write to your friends that ye are in health " (62b).

FRO (*passim*), from.

FRYING PAN, " out of the frying pan into the fire " (72c), from bad to worse.

FURTHER, (a) " might have gone further and fared worse " (62c), see next entry.
   (b) " the further ye go, the further behind " (88b), see previous entry.

GALLED, " Gup! with a galled back, Gill " (52d).

GALL, " rub him on the gall " (71b), *gall*=a sore, a rubbed place. " Enough, you rubbed the guiltie on the gaule."—*Mirr. for Mag.* (1559), 463.

GANDER, " not a more gaggling gander hence to Chester " (30d), cackling goose, a woman given to immoderate laughter and idle talk. " But when the priest is at seruice no man sitteth, but gagle and ducke like so many geese."—Hackluyt, *Voyages* (1582), i. 241.

GAPS, (*a*) " to stop two gaps with one bush " (95*a*), to do (or achieve) a double purpose : cf. " to kill two birds with one stone."

(*b*) " to stop gaps with rushes " (95*a*), a simile of futile effort.

GAT, " she gat a husband " (25*d*), got : an old preterite.

GAY, (*a*) " all thing is gay that is green " (54*a*), *green* = fresh, new, recent : cf. a green memory.

(*b*) " as we may we love to go gay " (27*a*).

GEAR, " ware that gear " (71*d*), *i.e.* be careful of that matter : *gear* formerly did service for not only dress or ornament, but for outfit of all kinds, goods, and property generally ; also matter, business, affair, &c. " I will remedy this gear ere long ! "—Shakspeare, 2 *Henry VI.* (1594), iii. 1.

GEAT, " nor nought we can geat " (11*a*), get : see the rhyme with " meat " in next line.

GENTLE, " farewell, gentle Godfrey " (36*b*).

GENTLEMAN, " Jack would be a gentleman if he could speak French " (35*b*) is obviously a relic of the Norman subversion of England. Speaking of the rule of the Anglo-Norman kings, the elder Disraeli writes :— " This was the time when it was held a shame among Englishmen to appear English. It became proverbial to describe a Saxon who ambitioned some distinguished rank, that " he would be a gentleman if he could but talk French."—*Amenities of Literature.*

GID, " such a gid did her head take " (40*c*), properly a disease in sheep, now known as " sturdy," marked by staggers, stupor, &c., and which is caused by an insect in the brain : hence *gid* here =" maggot," fancy, " bee in bonnet."

GIFT, (*a*) " throw no gift again at the giver's head " (37*c*), cf. " look no gift horse in the teeth."

(*b*) " as free of gift as a poor man of his eye " (37*d*).

GILL, wanton, strumpet : but the word, a common female name, does not always carry a bad meaning.

GINIFINEE, see Nycebecetur.

GIVE, " better to give than take " (13b), the usual form
is " better to give than to receive."

GLEANING, " thou goest a-gleaning ere the cart have
carried " (34b), *i.e.* you are " too previous "; you seek
a thing before it is lost.

GLOME, GLOMED, " did lower and glome " (23c)—" folks
glomed on me too " (23c), lour, look gloomy.

GOD, (a) " she is one of them to whom God bad ho ! "
(39d), *ho*=stop: formerly an exclamation to arrest
attention, and more particularly a call to cessation of
action : " *There is no ho with him* "=he is not to be
restrained.
    (b) " God is where he was " (46d).
    (c) " here is God in th' aumbry " (63d), (a) *aumbry*
=cupboard, pantry, almonry; specifically a room in
which alms were distributed; and (b) *ambry*=a niche
or cupboard near the altar in a church in which were
kept the utensils used for public worship; a slight
confusion exists between the two forms which, however, is of little moment.
    (d) " every man for himself and God for us all "
(96d).
    (e) " God is no botcher " (53b).
    (f) " alway the grace of God is worth a fair " (46c),
see Fair.
    (g) " out of God's blessing into the warm sun "
(167a), from bad to worse; " to jump out of the
frying-pan into the fire " : and conversely, " I am too
much i' the sun " (*Hamlet*, i. 2)=unfortunate, un-
blessed. " Therefore if thou wilt follow my advice, and
prosecute thine own determination, thou shalt come
out of a warme Sunne into God's blessing."—Lyly,
Euphues (1579), 23b. " Pray God they bring us not.
when all is done, Out of God's blessing into this
warm sun."—Harrington, *Epig.* (d. 1612), ii. 56.
    (h) " God sendeth cold after clothes " (11b). " Dieu
donne le froid selon la robbe," is the French form of
this proverb, found in *Les Prémices* (1594), by Henry
Estienne.
    (i) " God never sendeth mouth but he sendeth
meat " (11a).
    (j) " there was God . . . when all is done " (17c).

(k) " who hopeth in God's help his help cannot start " (11c), *start*=change, put aside, alter.
(l) " God stint all strife " (88d).
(m) " God have mercy, brother " (88d).
(n) " spend and God shall send " (66d).
(o) " God will send time to provide for time " (47b).
(p) " God and Saint Luke save you " (43a).

GODFREY, see Gentle.

GOETH, " as fast as one goeth another cometh " (*Epigrams*).

GOLD, (a) " all is not gold that glitters " (27c). " Uns proverbes dit et raconte Que tout n'est pas ors c'on voit luire."—*Li Diz de freire Denise cordelier* (c. 1300). "All things that shineth is not by and by pure gold."—Udall, *Ralph Roister Doister* (1566). See also Chaucer, *Chanones Yemannes Tale*, and Lydgate, *On the Mutability of Human Affairs*.
(b) " a man may buy gold too dear " (81c).
(c) " in words gold and whole " (77d), words of wisdom and import : the simile of golden speech is common, and on the other hand we have, " Speech is silvern, but silence is golden."

GOOD, (a) " of a good beginning cometh a good end " (25d). " But in proverbe I have herde saie, That who that well his warke beginneth, The rather a good ende he winneth."—Gower, *Confessio Amantis* (1393).
(b) " a man far from his good is nigh his harm " (91c).
(c) " they know no end of their good nor beginning of any goodness " (39c).
(d) " he knoweth none end of his good " (*Epigrams*).
(e) " to do me, not the more good, but the less harm " (24d)
(f) " may do her good and you no harm " (29a).
(g) " if he be good now, of his ill past no force " (33b), by repentance and well-doing forgiveness is won.
(h) " with many conditions good, one that is ill Defaceth the flower of all, and doth all spill " (76d), *i.e.* " the strength of a chain is that of its weakest link."
(i) " evil gotten good never proveth well " (42d).

(*j*) " her good be laid up so, lest thieves might spy it, that n'other she could, nor he can, come by it " (100*c*).

(*k*) " he that hath plenty of goods shall have more; He that hath but little, he shall have less ; He that hath right nought, right nought shall possess " (46*b*).

(*l*) " I hope good hap be not all outworn " (93*d*).

GOOD CHEAP, see Cheap.

GOODWIN SANDS, " set up shop upon Goodwin's sands " (92*c*), properly Godwin Sands, from Godwin Earl of Kent, the father of King Harold II. The land now represented by these quicksands (off the east coast of Kent) was given to the monastery of St. Augustin at Canterbury, but the abbot neglecting to keep the sea wall in repair, the tract was submerged about 1100.

GOOSE, (*a*) " the pure penitent that stole a goose and stuck down a feather " (42*c*).

(*b*) " as deep drinketh the goose as the gander " (82*d*), " what is good for the goose is good for the gander " is the modern version. " Gentlewoman, either you thought my wits very short, that a sip of wine could alter me, or else yours very sharp, to cut me off so roundly, when as I (without offence be it spoken) have heard, that as deepe drinketh the goose as the gander."—Lyly, *Euphues and his England.*

GOSLING, " who meddleth in all things may shoe the gosling " (59*d*), *i.e.* undertake a work of supereroga-tion, engage in a foolish or fruitless task. " Whoso melles of wat men dos, Let hym cum hier and shoo the ghos."—*Inscrip.* in Whalley Church (*c.* 1434). " What hath lay men to do The gray goose for to sho ! "—Skelton, *Colin Clout* (*c.* 1510). Compare " It is as great pyte to se a woman wepe as a gose to go barefote."—*Hundred Mery Talys* (*c.* 1525).

GOSPEL, " all is not gospel that thou dost speak " (57*a*), the exact truth.

GOTTEN, (*a*) " soon gotten, soon spent " (76*a*).

(*b*) " ill gotten, ill spent " (76*a*).

GRACE, " in space cometh grace " (11*a*), *i.e.* in time a condition of mind and conduct that embellishes char-acter and commands favour and esteem : cf. *past grace* =devoid of shame.

GRAFT, " then graft we a green graft on a rotten root "
(45*a*).

GRASS, " while the grass groweth the horse starveth "
(36*d*). " Whylst grass doth growe, oft sterves the
seely steede."—Whetstone, *Promos and Cassandra*
(1578). " Ay, sir, but, While the grass grows,—The
proverb is something musty."—Shakspeare, *Hamlet*
(1596), iii. 2.

GRATETH, " where this . . . gravely grateth " (6*b*),
touches, concerns, disturbs. " Grating so harshly all
his days of quiet."—Shakspeare, *Hamlet* (1596), iii. 1.

GREASE, " she fryeth in her own grease " (44*d*), to be
left vindictively or resentfully alone : also " stew in
one's own juice." " But certeynly I made folk such
chere That in his owne grees I made him frie."—
Chaucer, *Prologue of Wyf of Bathe.*

GREEDY, " they be both greedy guts all given to get "
(39*c*), gluttons. " *Edace*, an eater, a devourer, a
greedigut."—Florio, *Worlde of Wordes* (1598).

GREEVES, " lamenting their greeves " (47*a*), here shin
shackles or the stocks, with an eye on the old plural
of grief. An iron foot was formerly so-called (see
Mir. Mag. 46).

GROANING, " a groaning horse and a groaning wife
never fail their master " (60*c*), *groaning-wife*=a
woman ready to lie-in. " As smoothe as a groaning-
wive's bellie."—Nashe, *Unf. Trav.* (1594), 92 (Chis-
wick Press, 1892).

GROAT, (*a*) see Bestill.
    (*b*) " not worth a groat " (33*d*, 38*b*), a small stand-
ard of value ; *grey groat*=something of no value, a
" brass farthing." " I'll not leave him worth a grey
groat."—Marlowe, *Jew of Malta* (1586), iv. 4.
    (*c*) " who can sing so merry a note As may he that
cannot change a groat ? " (47*a*).

GROIN, " like a hog hangeth the groin on her husband "
(74*c*), *groin* (A.N.) = to grumble, and as subs. =
grumbler, malcontent : usually " groiner."

GROMWELL SEED, " fair words did fet gromwell seed
plenty " (53*c*), possibly with an eye on *gravelled*=

worried, vexed; gromwell seed being anciently administered for the cure of gravel.

GROUND, " these lovers . . . think the ground bear them not " (25c), *i.e.* in modern phrase, are " up in the skies," have neither eyes nor ears for aught than their mutual endearments.

GUEST, (a) " an unbidden guest knoweth not where to sit " (21b).

(b) " I bid you to dinner as no guest " (59a), *i.e.* without formality, to take " pot-luck," as we now have it. Or, it may be elliptical = " as we have no invited guests."

GYLES, " dread of such gyles " (48c), guiles, deceits. " Many on trowyn on here wylys, And many tymes the pye hem gylys."—*MS. Harl.* (1701), f. 3.

HAB OR NAB (9b), have or have not, without order, by fair means or foul.

HACKNEY-MEN (40b), originally proprietors of horses let for hire: *hackney* = a saddle horse. It was not until the reign of Charles I. that the title was transferred to the drivers of vehicles, the year 1625 being the date of the first appearance of hackney coaches in the streets of London. They were then only twenty in number, but the innovation occasioned an outcry (Sharman): " The world runs on wheeles. The hackney-men, who were wont to have furnished travellers in all places with fitting and serviceable horses for any journey, (by the multitude of coaches) are undone by the dozens, and the whole commonwealth most abominably jaded, that in many places a man had as good to ride on a wooden post, as to poast it upon one of those hunger-starv'd hirelings."—Taylor, *Works* (1630).

HAD, (a) " had I wist " (6c), had I known: a very common exclamation in old writers, who also used it substantively. " But, out alas, I wretch too late did sorrowe my amys, Unless lord Promos graunt me grace, in vayne is had-y-wist."—Whetstone, *Promos and Cassandra* (1578), ii. 2. " His pallid feares, his sorrows, his affrightings, His late-wisht had-I-wists, remorcefull bitings."—Browne, *Brit. Past.* (1613), I., ii. 57.

(*b*) " who had that he hath not would do that he
doeth not " (95*d*).

HADDOCK, (*a*) " not worth a haddock " (99*d*), of small
value : cf. " as witty as a haddock "=downright foolish (*Hickscorner* [*c.* 1550], E.E.D.S., *Anon. Plays,*
Ser. 1, 153*b*).

(*b*) " thus had he brought haddock to paddock "
(99*d*), outrun the constable : *haddock = cod =* purse
(" the fish we call a hadock, or a cod " [Florio])—
the meaning thus being, a purse or bag of money
has melted as if cast to the paddocks (frogs).

HAIR, (*a*) " make his hair grow through his hood "
(66*b*), *i.e.* go-betweens will become rivals : usually the
phrase means " to cuckold." " It will make his hair
grow through his hood."—Ingelend, *Disobedient Child*
(*c.* 1550), *Works* (E.E.D.S.), 74*b*. " French hood,
French hood, I will make your hair grow thorough."
—Middleton, *Anything for a Quiet Life* (1662).

(*b*) " long hair and short wit " (82*d*). " Hair ! 'tis
the basest stubble ; in scorn of it The proverb sprung,
—He has more hair than wit."—Decker, *Satiromastix*
(1602). " More hair than wit,—it may be ; I'll prove
it : The cover of the salt hides the salt, and therefore
it is more than the salt : the hair, that covers the
wit, is more than the wit, for the greater hides the
less."—Shakspeare, *Two Gentlemen of Verona* (1595),
iii. 2.

(*c*) " take a hair from his beard " (78*d*).

HALF, (*a*) " this half sheweth what the whole meaneth "
(84*d*).

(*b*) " that's just if the half shall judge the whole "
(50*a*).

(*c*) " half warned, half armed " (77*a*), the modern
version is " forewarned, forearmed."

HALL, " it is merry in hall when beards wag all " (79*d*),
an extremely popular saying in olden times. " 'It is
merry in hall when beards wag all.' Husband, for
this, these words to mind I call : This is meant by
men, in their merry eating, Not to wag their beards
in brawling and threating.—Wife, the meaning hereof
differeth not two pins, Between wagging of men's
beards and women's chins."—Heywood, *Works*

(E.E.D.S.), ii. 167*b.* " Be merry, be merry, my wife
has all, For women are shrews, both short and tall,
'Tis merry in hall when beards wag all."—Shakspeare, 2 *Henry IV.* (1598), v. 3.

HALFPENNY, see Hand.

HALVES, " as for that, reason runneth to halves—As
well for the cow calf as for the bull " (62*a*), see
Cow-calf.

HALTER, " thy taking of thine halter in thine arms
teacheth other to beware of their harms by thine "
(42*b*).

HAND, (*a*) " so hard is your hand set on your halfpenny " (14*c*), eye on main chance, attention riveted
on self-interest. " *Ri.* Dromio, looke heere, now is
my hand on my half-peny. *Half.* Thou liest, thou
hast not a farthing to lay thy hands on."—Lyly,
Mother Bombie (1594).

(*b*) " by your hand on your heart " (101*c*), as a
symbol of sincerity.

(*c*) " glad is he that hath her in hand " (52*d*), under
control.

(*d*) " many hands make light work " (66*b*). " The
werke is the soner done that hathe many handes :
Many handys make light werke : my leve child."—
How the Goode Wif Thaught hir Doughter (*c.* 1471),
113.

(*e*) " both their hands full " (73*c*).

(*f*) " she can play on both hands " (24*b*), is expert,
" wide."

HANG, (*a*) " he that hangeth himself a Sunday, Shall
hang still uncut down a Monday for me " (33*b*).

(*b*) " hang the bell about the cat's neck " (38*d*),
see *infra.* " But they are loth to mell, and loth to
hang the bell about the cat's neck, for dread to have
a check."—Skelton, *Colin Clout* (*c.* 1518), 165. " But,
quoth one Mouse unto the rest, Which of us all dare
be so stout To hang the bell cat's neck about? If
here be any, let him speake. Then all replide, We
are too weake : The stoutest Mouse and tallest Rat
Doe tremble at a grim-fac'd Cat."—*Diogines Lan-
thorne* (1607).

HANGED, " he that hath an ill name is half hanged "
(77a), or modern, " give a dog a bad name and hang
him."

HANGING, see Wedding.

HAP, (a) " such hap here hapt " (48c)—" brought by good
hap " (75c), chance, fortune : subs. or verb.
(b) " in hope of good hap " (100c), see *supra*.

HAPPY, (a) " happy man, happy dole " (9d), a generic
wish for success. " Wherein, happy man be his dole,
I trust that I Shall not speede worst, and that very
quickly."—Edwards, *Damon and Pith., O. Pl.* (Reed),
i. 177.
(b) " better be happy then wise " (75c).

HARDLY, " hardly if ye can " (59c), boldly, certainly.
" And hardly, aungel, trust therto, For doughtles it
shal be do."—*MS. Coll. Trin. Dubl.* D. iv. 18.

HARE, (a) " there goeth the hare away " (13a), *i.e.*
" that's the gist, trend, secret, why and wherefore of
the matter." " *Man.* By my fayth a lytell season
I folowd the counsell and dyet of reason. *Gets.*
There went the hare away."—Medwall, *Nature* (1510).
(b) " to hold with the hare and run with the
hounds " (24a), play a double game, keep on good
terms with two contending parties.
(c) " mad as a March hare " (73a), a proverbial
type of madness ; but Skelton has it differently.
" Thanne they begynne to swere and to stare, And
be as braynles as a Marshe hare."—*Blowbol's Test*
(14—?). " As mery as a Marche hare."—Skelton,
Magn. (1526), 930. " I saye, thou madde Marche
hare."—Skelton, *Replycation Against Certayne Yong
Scolers* (1520).
(d) " catch (or hunt for) a hare with a taber " (21a),
to engage ir or attempt a hopeless task : the taber
was a shallow drum beaten with the fingers. " The
poore man that gives but his bare fee, or perhaps
pleads *in formâ pauperis*, he hunteth for hares with
a taber, and gropeth in the darke to find a needle in
a botle of hay."—Greene, *Quip for an Upstart Courtier* (1592), *Harl. Misc.*, v. 407. " One day after the
set of this comet men shall catch hares with tabers."

—Simon Smel-knave, *Fearefull and Lamentable Effects of Two Dangerous Comets* (1591).

(*e*) " set the hare's head against the goose jiblet " (64*a*). " Ide set mine old debts against my new driblets, And the hare's foot against the goose giblets."—Decker, *Shomakers Holiday* (1600).

HARM, (*a*) " there is no harm done in all this fray, Neither pot broken nor water spilt " (44*c*).

(*b*) " thou art so wooed thou knowest not who doth thee harm, who doth thee good " (86*c*).

(*c*) " it is good to beware by other men's harms " (42*b*).

HARP, (*a*) " ye harp on the string that giveth no melody " (63*d*), dwell persistently : see *infra*.

(*b*) " harp no more on that string " (96*d*), see *supra*.

HARPERS, " have among you blind harpers " (79*b*), a proverbial pledge in drinking. Macaulay observes that in the old ballad poetry, all the gold is " red " and all the ladies " gay." So, also, the harpers are blind. *The Poet's Blind Man's Bough: or, Have among you blinde Harpers,* was the title of a tract by Martin Parker, printed in 1651. " *Leoc.* Have towards thee, Philotas. *Phil.* To thee, Archippus. *Arch.* To thee, Molops. *Molops.* Have among you, blind fiddlers."—Cartwright, *Royall Slave* (1651).

HARVEST, " a long harvest for a little corn " (46*c*).

HASTE, (*a*) " haste maketh waste " (60*c*).

(*b*) " the more haste the less speed " (7*a*).

(*c*) " in more haste than good speed " (20*b*).

(*d*) " no haste but good " (97*c*).

(*e*) " then seeth he haste and wisdom things far odd " (7*a*).

HASTY, " the hasty man never wanteth woe " (7*b*). " Thou wert afire to be a ladie, and now your ladiship and you may both blowe at the cole, for aught I know. ' Selfe doe, selfe have.' ' The hastie man never wanteth woe,' they say."—Jonson, &c., *Eastward Hoe* (1605), v. 1.

HAT, " mine old hat must have a new band " (52*d*).

HATCHET, " I have hanged up my hatchet " (33*b*).

HATH BEEN, " ye know what he hath been . . . ye know not what he is " (37*d*).

HAUT, " men haut or high " (81*d*), *haut*=proud. " No lord of thine, thou haught insulting man."—Shakspeare, *Richard II.* (1597), iv. 1.

HAWK, (*a*) " she hath one point of a good hawk, she is hardy " (64*b*), bold, stubborn.
(*b*) " he hath his hawks in the mew, but With empty hands men may no hawks allure " (66*b*), *mew* =a place where falcons were kept.

HAWKING, (*a*) " the first point of hawking is hold fast " (64*b*).
(*b*) " hawking upon me, his mind herein to break " (18*a*), spluttering, spitting : *hawk* is from Welsh " hochi," apparently an imitative word (Skeat).

HEAD, (*a*) " then have you his head fast under your girdle " (71*b*), on the hip, " in chancery."
(*b*) " break my head and then give me a plaster " (95*b*).
(*c*) " a scabbed head is soon broken " (60*b*).
(*d*) " my aching head to ease I will couch a hogshead " (58*b*), see Couch.
(*e*) " when the head acheth, all the body is the worse " (85*d*).
(*f*) " their heads full of bees " (47*c*), projects : usually denotive, however, of crazy crotchets.
(*g*) see Nail.
(*h*) " to-morrow I will to my beads to pray that as ye both will, so ache your heads " (58*a*).
(*i*) " so many heads, so many wits " (9*c*). " Quot homines tot sententiæ " (Terence).   " For amonge feaders are alwayes sondry appetytes, and in great assemblyes of people, dyvurse, and varyaunt judgements ; as the saynge is, so many heades, so many wyttes."—Queen Elizabeth, *Godly Meditacyon of the Christen Sowle* (1548). " Ah, sirha, I see wel the olde proverbe is true, which saith : so many men so many mindes."—Gascoigne, *Glasse of Government* (1575).
(*k*) " two heads are better than one " (23*d*).

HEALING, " it is ill healing of an old sore " (87*c*).

HEALTH, " ye may write to your friends that ye are in health " (62b).

HEAR, (a) " a man should hear all parts, ere he judge any " (49b).
 (b) " I cannot hear on that side " (*Epigrams*), an excuse for wilful deafness.

HEART, (a) " to set at my heart that thou settest at thy heel " (34b).
 (b) " she taketh such heart of grace " (87c), to pick up courage, some thinking it was originally " to take heart at grass ": in the *Epigrams on Proverbs* (92) both forms occur—" thou takest heart of grass . . . not heart of grace." " He came within the castle wall to-day, His absence gave him so much heart of grace, Where had my husband been but in the way, He durst not," &c.—Harington, *Ariost.* (1591), xxi. 39.
 (c) " your heart is in your hose " (36d), a simile of fear or trepidation : modern, " heart in mouth " or " shoes." " Be your hearts in your hose? "— *Thersites, Anon. Pl.*, Ser. 1 (E.E.D.S.), 208a.

HEAVEN, (a) " she made us cheer heaven high " (60r), heartily, " sky-high," " raise the roof."
 (b) see Hell.

HEDGE, " where the hedge is lowest, men may soonest over " (68d). " Where hedge is lowe, there every man treads downe, And friendship failes, when Fortune list to frowne."—Gascoigne, *Posies* (1575).

HEED, " take heed is a fair thing " (88c).

HEELS, " show (or take to) a fair pair of heels " (78b), to take flight, run away. " Darest thou be so valiant as to play the coward with thy indenture and show it a fair pair of heels? "—Shakspeare, 1 *Henry IV.* (1598), ii. 4.

HEINSBY (38a), upstart, " nouveau riche "; a generic reproach of any person in an inferior grade of society, or of low origin : cf. *rudesby*=an impertinent.

HEKST, " when bale is hekst, boot is next " (46c), things when at their worst begin to mend. " When bale is greatest, then is bote a nie bore."—Chaucer, *Testament of Love.* " When the bale is hest, Thenne is the bote nest, Quoth Hendyng."—*Proverbs of Hendyng*, MS. (*c*. 1320).

HEN, "as nice as a nun's hen" (52*c*), a very ancient proverbial simile : ? *nun*=(*a*) a variety of pigeon having its head almost covered with a veil of feathers ; (*b*) the smew ; or (*c*) the blue titmouse—most likely the last. "Women, women, love of women, Make bare purs with some men. Some be nyse as a nonne hene, Yet al thei be not soo ; Some be lewde, some all be schrewde, Go schrewes wher thei goo."—*Satirical Verses on Women* (1462). "I have the taught dyvysyon between Frende of effect, and frende of countenaunce ; The nedeth not the gall of none hen That cureth eyen."—Lydgate, *Proverbes* (*c*. 1520). "I knewe a priest that was as nice as a Nonnes Henne."—Wilson, *Arte of Rhetorique* (1562).

HEPT, "this hall hept with gold" (36*a*), heaped.

HEREAFTER, "though hereafter come not yet" (82*a*).

HEW, "hew not too high lest the chips fall in thine eye" (82*a*). "For an old proverbe it is ledged ' he that heweth to hie, with chips he may lose his sight.'"—Chaucer, *Testament of Love*.

HIGH, (*a*) "not too high for the pie, nor too low for the crow" (82*a*).
(*b*) see Hew.
(*c*) "her heart is full high when her eye is full low" (28*a*).

HILT, "I will be as soon hilt" (44*c*), probably =cudgelled : *hilt*=cudgel.

HIP, "then have ye him on the hip or on the hurdle" (71*b*), at an advantage : probably from hunting (Nares) ; the hurdle in old law was a frame or sledge on which criminals were drawn from the prison to the place of execution, and designed to preserve the offender from the extreme torment of being dragged on the ground. "I'll have our Michael Cassio on the hip."—Shakspeare, *Othello* (1602), ii. 7.

HO, "to whom God bade Ho!" (39*d*), originally a call or exclamation ; hence a stop or limit, and whence many idioms—*out of all ho*=out of all bounds ; *no ho*

with him = not to be restrained ; *Let us ho* = stop.
" Howbeit they would not crie hoa here, but sent in
post some of their covent to Rome? "—Stanihurst,
Description of Ireland, 26.

HOG, (*a*) " routing like a hog " (30*a*), *rout* = snore.
" Hark, my pygg, how the knave dooth rowte ! Well,
whyle he sleepth in Idlenes lappe, Idlenes marke on
hym shall I cappe."—*Wit and Science* (E.E.D.S.,
Anon. Pl., Ser. 4).

(*b*) " every man basteth the fat hog, but the lean
shall burn ere he basted be " (46*a*).

(*c*) " cast precious stones before hogs " (93*a*), a
variant of " to cast pearls before swine."

HOLD, (*a*) " hold fast when ye have it " (29*c*), " sit
tight," " freeze to."

(*b*) " hold ye fast . . . lest ye be cast " (64*b*).

(*c*) " who may hold that will away " (75*d*).

(*d*) [She will] "let fall her hold [rather] than be
too bold " (64*b*).

HOLYDAY, (*a*) " this geare was gotten on a holyday "
(75*d*).

(*b*) " he laid up for holydays " (100*c*).

HOME, (*a*) " home is homely though it be poor " (11*b*).

(*b*) " thou gossipest at home, to meet me at land's
end " (83*a*).

HONESTY, " the flower of honesty " (28*b*), cf. " flower
of chivalry," " flower of the flock," &c.

HONEY, " where words seemed honey . . . now are
they mustard " (54*b*).

HOOD, " by my hood " (102*d*), formerly, as now, the
commonest as well as the most sacred things were
convenient pegs upon which to hang a " cussword."

HOOK, (*a*) " avale, unhappy hook " (44*a*), adieu : *hook* =
a term of reproach, here equivalent to " miserable
failure." " That unhappy hook."—Heywood, *Works*
(E.E.D.S.), I., 26*c* and 35*d*.

(*b*) " by hook or by crook " (44*a*), by some means
or other, by fair means or foul, at all hazards : a
term derived from old forestry. " Nor will suffer this
boke, By hooke or by crooke, Prynted for to be."—
Skelton, *Colin Clout* (1520). " Dynmure Wood was

ever open and common to the . . . inhabitants of
Bodmin . . . to bear away upon their backs a burden
of lop, crop, hook, crook, and bag wood."—*Bodmin
Register* (1525).

HOP-ON-MY-THUMB, " it is a small hop on my thumb "
(31*b*), a small, insignificant person : in derision.
" Plain friend hop o' my thumb, know you who we
are? "—Shakspeare, *Taming of the Shrew* (1593).

HOPPETH, " when wooers hop in and out, long time
may bring him that hoppeth best, at last to have
the ring " (9*a*).

HORN WOOD (99*c*), *i.e.* horn-mad, stark staring mad
because cuckolded ; see Wood. " Sure my mistress is
horn-mad."—Shakspeare, *Comedy of Errors* (1593),
ii. 1.

HORSE, (*a*) " rub a galled horse on the back and he
will kick " (*Epigrams*), see next entry.
　　(*b*) " I rub the galled horse back till he winch "
(84*c*), *winch* = wince.
　　(*c*) " a scald horse is good enough for a scabb'd
squire " (40*b*), *i.e.* like to like ; a mangy screw is
good enough for a disreputable rider : " scald " and
" scabb'd " are synonymous, and both are used in
contempt of anything shabby, disgusting, or paltry.
" Like lettuce like lips, a scab'd horse for a scald
squire."—*New Custom, Anon. Pl.*, Ser. 1 (E.E.D.S.),
174*d*.
　　(*d*) " a short horse is soon curried " (23*b*).
　　(*e*) " a man may well lead a horse to the water, but
he cannot make him drink " (33*a*).
　　(*f*) " it be a good horse that never stumbleth " (20*a*).
" A good horse that trippeth not once in a journey."
—*Three Proper and Wittie Familiar Letters* (1580).
　　(*g*) " some man may steal a horse better than some
other may stand and look upon " (91*d*). " Good Epi,
let mee take a nap ; for as some man may better
steale a horse then another looke over a hedge ; so
divers shall be sleepie when they would fainest take
rest."—Lyly, *Endimion* (1591).
　　(*h*) " it is . . . a proud horse that will not bear
his own provender " (98*b*). " Sir, hee's a proud horse
that will not carry his own provander, I warrant yee."
—Porter, *Two Angry Women of Abingdon* (1599).

HEY. PROV.　　　　　　　　　　　　　M

(*i*) " recover the horse, or lose the saddle too " (95*a*).

(*j*) " no man ought to look a given horse in the mouth " (13*c*). " A gyven hors may not be loked in the tethe."—*Vulgaria Stambrigi* (*c.* 1510). " It is certainly as old as Jerome, a Latin father of the fourth century; who when found fault with . . . quoted the proverb, that it did not behove to look a gift horse in the mouth."—Trench, *Proverbs and their Lessons.*

(*k*) " as shortly as a horse will lick his ear " (93*d*).

(*l*) " it would have made a horse break his halter " (53*d*).

(*m*) " God have mercy, horse " (78*c*), *i.e.* God help us ; according to *Tarlton's Jests* (1611), this arose from an adventure of Richard Tarleton, the player, with Banks's performing horse, Morocco, the phrase being a retort that tickled the ears of the assembled crowd and " caught on."

(*n*) " the grey mare is the better horse " (64*a*), the wife is master : a tradition, perhaps, of the time when priests were forbidden to carry arms or ride on a male horse : *Non enim licuerate pontificem sacrorum vel arma ferre, vel praeter quam in equuâ equitare.*— Beda, *Hist. Eccl.* ii. 13. Fr. *Mariage d'épervier*=a hawk's marriage ; the female hawk being the larger and stronger bird. Lord Macaulay's explanation (preference given to the grey mares of Flanders over the finest coach horses of England) is the merest guesswork. " What ! shall the graye mayre be the better horse, And the wanton styll at home? "—*Pryde and Abuse of Women Now a Dayes* (*c.* 1550).

(*o*) " evermore the common horse is worst shod " (42*a*), cf, " the shoemaker's wife is worst shod."

(*p*) " folk call on the horse that will carry alway " (42*a*), in modern phrase, " the willing horse is always most ridden."

(*q*) " as wholesome a morsel for my comely corse as a shoulder of mutton for a sick horse " (85*a*), utterly worthless, distasteful. " Counsel to him is as good as a shoulder of mutton to a sick horse."— Jonson, *Every Man in his Humour* (1596), ii. 1.

HORSE LOAVES, " as high as two horse loaves her person is " (24*c*), a jocular standard of measurement (sometimes three horse loaves) : compare the phrase still current which says that diminutive persons must stand on three penny loaves to look over the back of a goat, or a duck. The horse-loaf was made of beans and wheat. " Her stature scant three horse loaves did exceed."—Harington, *Ariosto*.

HORSE PLUM, " purple ruddy like a horse plum " (24*c*), *horse*, a generic qualificative=coarse, large.

HOSE, " your heart is in your hose " (36*d*), see Heart. " *Primus Pastor*, Breck outt youre voce, let se as ye yelp. *Tercius Pastor*. I may not for the pose bot I have help. *Secundus Pastor*. A, thy hert is in thy hose."—*Towneley Mysteries* (*c*. 1430).

HOST, see Reckoners.

HOT, (*a*) " hot love soon cold " (6*d*). " Dowghter, in this I can thinke none oother But that it is true thys proverbe old, Hastye love is soone hot and soone cold ! "—*Wyt and Science* (*c*. 1540), *Anon. Pl.*, Ser. 4.
(*b*) " when th' iron is hot, strike," see Iron.
(*c*) " little pot soon hot," see Pot.

HOUSE, " a man may love his house well though he ride not on the ridge " (61*a*).

HOUSEHOLDERS, see Wishers.

HOUSEWIFE, " a clean-fingered housewife and an idle " (26*c*), *i.e.* if a mistress does her duty she cannot ever have clean hands.

HUNDRED, " what ye won in the hundred ye lose in the shire " (92*b*), *hundred*=a division of a county in England, supposed to be named from originally containing one hundred families of freemen.

HUNGER, (*a*) " hunger droppeth over out of both their noses " (39*d*).
(*b*) " hunger pierceth stone wall " (47*a*). " They said, they were an-hungry ; sigh'd forth proverbs ;— That, hunger broke stone walls ; that, dogs must eat ; That, meat was made for mouths ; that, the gods sent not corn for the rich man only."—Shakspeare, *Coriolanus* (1610), i. 1.
(*c*) " hunger maketh hard beans sweet " (29*b*), cf. " hunger is the best sauce."
(*d*) " they must hunger in frost, that will not work in heat " (34*d*).

M 2

(*e*) " two hungry meals made the third a glutton " (45*b*).

HUNTER, " close hunting the good hunter alloweth " (72*a*).

HUSBANDS, " husbands are in heaven whose wives scold not " (85*c*).

HUSWIFE (25*a*), primarily a housewife : whence (*a*) domestic servant ; (*b*) a wanton or a gad-about wench ; and (*c*) a comic endearment. Hence, too, " housewifery " and " housewife's tricks "=the habit of wantonness. " A gude husy-wife ay rinning in the toun."—*Gawain and Gologras,* " Ballade " (1508), Pinkerton, *Scottish Poems* (1792), iii. " Half lost for lack of a good huswife's looking to."—Puttenham, *English Poesie* (1589), ii. 16 (ed. Arber, 148). " Huswife, I'll have you whipped for slandering me."—*Look About You* (1600), sc. 28 (Dodsley, *Old Plays,* 4th ed., 1875, vii. 476).

IGNORANCY, " cometh not of ignorancy " (73*b*), ignorance. " Rocked in blyndnes and ignorauncy."—Tyndall, *Workes,* 157.

ILES, see Out isles.

ILL, (*a*) " from ill to worse and worse " (89*a*), the modern version is " bad to worse."
(*b*) " of two ills choose the least " (12*d*). " Of harmes two the lesse is for to cheese."—Chaucer, *Troilus and Creseide.*
(*c*) " turn . . . ill beginning to a good end " (89*c*).
(*d*) " ill believed and worse heard " (91*b*).
(*e*) " they that think none ill are soonest beguiled " (73*d*).
(*f*) " all be not a-bed that shall have ill rest " (86*d*).
(*g*) " an ill wind that bloweth no man to good " (93*c*).

IMPORTABLE, " may grow importable " (82*b*), unendurable, insupportable. " Beware of the importable burdens of the high-mynded pharisees."—Bale, *English Votaries,* pt. i.

IN, " in by the week " (84*b*), see Week.

INCH, (a) " as good is an inch as an ell " (95c), *ell =* a cloth measure (in England 45 inches) : cf. " it is the first step that counts."

(b) " when I gave you an inch ye took an ell, till both ell and inch be gone " (95c), see *supra* (a).

(c) " better an inch of your will than an ell of your thrift " (95b), see *supra* (a).

(d) " an inch breaketh no square " (*Epigrams*).

INK, " ink is all black and hath an ill smack, No man will it drink or eat " (63a).

INN, " to take mine ease in mine inn " (12d), to enjoy oneself as if one were at home. " Shall I not take mine ease in mine inn, but I shall have my pocket picked ? "—Shakspeare, 1 *Henry IV.* (1598), iii. 3.

INSTEP, " high in th'instep " (37d), haughty, proud. " The gentleman was grown higher in the instep, as appeared by the insolent conditions he required."— Moryson, *Itin.* (1617), ii. 26. " He was too high in the instep to wear another man's shoes."—Fuller, *Holy War* (1639), II. viii. (1647), 53.

IRON, " when the iron is hot strike " (8c), act at the appropriate time. " Right so as while that iron is hot, men should strike."—Chaucer, *Melib.* (c. 1386), 70.

ITCH, " itch and ease can no man please " (62b).

ITCHING, " he whom in itching no scratching will forbear, he must bear the smarting that shall follow there " (28c).

IWYS (*passim*), certainly, indeed, truly : often no more than a metrical tag.

JACK, (a) " jack out of office " (58d), one dismissed or out of employment. " For liberalitie is tourned Jacke out of office, and others appointed to have the custodie."—Rich, *Farewell to Militarie Profession* (1581).

(b) " all shall be well, Jack shall have Gill " (58c), Jack and Gill are generic for " man " and " woman " : specifically of the common people. " For Jok nor for Gyll will I turne my face."—*Townley Myst.* (c. 1460), iii. 336.

(c) " I have been common Jack to all that whole flock " (41d), in disparagement ; *i.e.* at everyone's beck and call : cf. " a twangling jack " (*Taming of the Shrew*), and " silken, sly, insinuating jacks " (*Richard III*.).

JERMAN, " just as Jerman's lips " (56*b*). " As just as German's lips, which came not together by nine mile."—Latimer, *Remaines*. " Agree like Dogge and Catte, and meete as just as German's lippes."—Gosson, *Schole of Abuse.*

JESTING, " it is ill jesting on the sooth " (88*a*), *i.e.* true jesting is no jest at all : *sooth* = truth.

JET, *subs.* and *verb* (*passim*), strut, swagger, pose. " O peace ! Contemplation makes a rare turkey-cock of him ; how he jets under his advanc'd plumes ! "—Shakspeare, *Twelfth Night* (1602), ii. 5.

JOAN (OR JONE), " ye should have none for Jone " (96*c*), *Joan* = a generic name for a female rustic. " Some men must love my lady, and some Joan."—Shakspeare, *Love's Labour Lost* (1588), iii. 1. 207.

JOHN DRAWLATCH (88*c*), a thief ; also idle fellow, loafer, ne'er-do-well. " Well, phisitian, attend in my chamber heere, till Stilt and I returne ; and if I pepper him not, say I am not worthy to be cald a duke, but a drawlatch."—Chettle, *Hoffman* (1602).

JOY, (*a*) " for one month's joy, to bring her whole life sorrow " (27*c*), in allusion to the honeymoon.
(*b*) " poverty brought that joy to joyfail " (100*c*).
(*c*) " with all your joy join all your jeopardy " (101*c*).

JOYFAIL, " poverty brought that joy to joyfail " (100*c*), *joyfail* = a nonce word intended as a pun.

JUDICARE, " to know how Judicare came into the Creed " (20*b*).

KA, " ka me, ka thee " (41*c*), a phrase implying mutual help, service, flattery and the like. " To keep this rule, kaw me and I kaw thee."—Lodge, *Fig for Momus* (1595), Sat. 1.

KEY, (*a*) " cold as a key " (54*b*), as cold as may be, spec. cold as in death : usually " key-cold." " With quaikard voce and hart cald as a key."—Douglas,

Pal. Hon. (1501), 674. " Poor key-cold figure of a holy king."—Shakspeare, *Richard III.* (1597), i. 2.

(*b*) " the keys hang not all by one man's girdle " (37*a*).

KID, " a piece of a kid is worth two of a cat " (86*a*).

KIND, " kind will creep where it may not go " (33*c*), *kind*=human nature, kinship. " He . . . rode in poste to his kynsman . . . verefiying the old proverbe : kynne will crepe, where it maie not go."—Hall, *Chron.* (*c.* 1548), *Edw. IV.*, 190. " Ay, gentle Thurio ; for you know that love Will creep in service when it cannot go."—Shakspeare, *Two Gentlemen of Verona* (1595), iv. 2.

KINSFOLK, " many kinsfolk, few friends " (45*d*).

KIRTLE, " though nigh be my kirtle yet near is my smock " (28*d*), *kirtle*=originally a man's garment reaching to the knees or lower, sometimes the only body garment, but more usually worn with a shirt (or smock) beneath, and a cloak or mantle above ; also (as here) a woman's gown : both forms became archaic long since. " Beside, there is a antiquitie a proverb no lesse practised then common, which is, Nearer unto mee is my shirt then my coate ; by following of which, every man commonly loveth his owne profit more than others."—*The Contention betweene Three Brethren ; the Whore-monger, the Drunkard, and the Dice Player* (1608).

KISS, (*a*) " many kiss the child for the nurse's sake " (84*d*).

(*b*) " how can she give a kiss, sour or sweet? Her chin and her nose within half an inch meet " (53*a*).

KNACKS, " such knacks in her bouget " (75*b*), see Bouget.

KNAVE, (*a*) " two false knaves need no broker " (35*d*), *broker*=a go-between. " Some will say, A crafty knave need no broker, But here's a craftie knave and a broker too."—*Knacke to Knowe a Knave* (1594). " As two false knaves need no Broker, for they can easily enough agree in wickednesse . . . so among true and faithfull men, there need no others."—*A Sword against Swearers* (1611).

(b) " an old knave is no child " (58a), see *infra*.
" Thus the English proverb saith, No knave to the
learned knave."—Moryson, *Itin.* (1627), iii. 5.

(c) " an old knave is no babe " (*Epigrams*), see
supra.

(d) " the one knave now croucheth while the other
craveth " (36a).

(e) " it is merry when knaves meet " (35d). " No
more of Cocke now I wryte, But mery it is when
knaves done mete."—*Cocke Lorelles Bote* (c. 1510).
" Merrie meeting? why that Title is stale. There's
a Boke cald Tis merry when knaves meete, and
there's a Ballad Tis merry when Malt-men meete;
and besides 'there's an old Proverbe The more the
merrier."—Samuel Rowlands, *Tis Merrie when Gossips meete* (1602).

(f) " the more knaves the worse company " (36a).

KNOWLEDGE, " I know and knowledge " (26a), own,
acknowledge, confess. " They knowledge thee to be
the Father of an infinite majesty."—*Goodly Primer*
(1535), 82 (1834).

KNUCKLEBONYARD, " he is a knucklebonyard " (40b), a
clumsy fellow. " A knokylbonyarde wyll counterfete
a clarke, He wolde trotte gentylly, but he is to
stark."—Skelton, *Magn.* (1526), 485.

LABOUR, " ye shall never labour younger " (21c), become, grow : cf. *to labour on* = to go on.

LABOURETH, " reason laboureth will " (13b), cultivates.

LACK, (a) " lack is the loss of these two young fools "
(49b).

(b) " no lack to lack a wife " (103a).

(c) " ye had been lost to lack your lust " (32c),
lust = wish, desire.

LADY, " there is nothing that agree'th worse than a
lady's heart and a beggar's purse " (27b).

LAMB, " look like a lamb " (91c).

LAMBSKIN, (a) " as soon goeth the young lamb's skin to
the market as the old ewe's " (60c). " It is a common saying, there do come as many skins of calves

to the market as there do of bulls or kine."—Barclay,
Ship of Fools (1509).

(*b*) "a lambskin . . . to lap her in " (76*c*), *i.e.*
beat, trounce her: *lambskin*=stroke, blow; *lap*=
coil, wind round, wrap up (cf. " The Wife Lapped in
Mowelles Skin," *Earl. Pop. Poet.*, iv. 179). "And
because therof, I did give her three or four lamb-
skines with the yerd. Thou servedst her well ynough,
said he."—*MS. Ashmol.*, 208.

LAP, see Lambskin (*b*).

LARUM (78*b*), hubbub, uproar. " Then the crye and
larum began."—Berners, *Huon* (*c.* 1533), cxxix. 472.

LAST, " he that cometh last make all fast ": (*Epigrams*).

LATE, (*a*) ": better late than never " (26*b*). " Far bet
than never is late."—Chaucer, *Can. Yeom. Prol. and
T.* (*c.* 1386), 857. Also in Tusser's *Five Hundred
Points of Good Husbandry.*

(*b*) " too late . . . this repentance shewed is "
(26*b*).

LAUGH, " they laugh that win " (10*d* and *Epigrams*),
the adage occurs in various forms: " they win that
laugh "; " they laugh best that laugh last "; " give
losers leave to talk," &c. " Give loosers leave to
talke : it is no matter what *sic probo* and his pennilesse companions prate, whilst we have the gold in
our coffers."—Nash, *Pierce Penilesse* (1592). " Let
them laugh that win the prize."—May, *Heir* (1622),
iii. 1.

LAUGHING, " from laughing to lowering " (54*c*).

LAUGHTER, " better is the last smile then the first
laughter " (94*d*), see Laugh.

LAWN, " he that will sell lawn before he can fold it, he
shall repent him before he have sold it " (19*b*).
Another " lawn " proverb says, " No piece of lawn so
pure but hath some fret " (Barnefield, *Pecunia*, 1598,
xxxvi.).

LAY, (*a*) " reason for reason ye so stiffly lay by proverb
for proverb " (14*d*), compare with " They conferre
the one with the other, and lay them with the lawe."
—*Tr. Bullinger's Decades* (1577), II. viii. 192.

(*b*) " the trial thereof we will lay a water till we

try more " (10a), put aside, defer judgment concerning, render nugatory : see Water. " If he had broke his arme . . . either Apollo must have played Bonesetter, or every occupation beene laide a water."— Gosson, *Schoole of Abuse* (1579).

LEAF, " she will turn the leaf " (64b), adopt a different line of conduct : now, always in a good sense. " He must turn the leaf and take out a new lesson."— Holinshed, *Chron.* (1577), I. 21 2.

LEAN, " lean is light " (25a).

LEAP, " look ere ye leap " (7c). " He that leaps before he look . . . may leap in the mire."—*Marr. Wit and Science* (c. 1570), *Anon. Plays* (E.E.D.S.), Ser. 4.

LEATHER, " they cut large thongs of other men's leather " (66b), cf. " to steal another man's thunder." " Men cut large thongs here of other men's leather." —Mary Paston, *Paston Letters* (1460), III. 372. " D'autrui cuir font large curoie."—*C'est li Mariages des Filles au Dyable*, MS. (c. 1300).

LEAVE, (a) " leave it or it leave you " (*Epigrams*).
(b) " better leave than lack " (12c). " A worthy work (wherein the Reader may rather leave then lack)."—*Fuller, Holy and Prof. State* (1642), IV. xiv. 310.

LECTOUR, " a wise lectour " (84a), a college or university " reader " or lecturer.

LEG, (a) " while the leg maimeth the boot harmeth " (56a).
(b) " a leg of a lark is better than is the body of a kite " (11b). " *Gyrtrude.* I would not change husbands with my sister ; I. ' The legge of a larke is better than the body of a kite.' *Mistress Touchstone.* Know that ; but—— *Gyrtrude.* What, sweet mother, what? *Mistress Touchstone.* It's but ill food when nothing's left but the claw."—Chapman, Marston, and Jonson, *Eastward Hoe* (1605).
(c) " in house to keep houshold, when folks will need wed, more things belong than four bare legs in a bed " (19c). " Furthermore it shall be lawful for him that marries without money to find four bare legs in a bed : and he that is too prodigal in spend-

ing, shall die a beggar by the statute."—*Pennilesse Parliament of Threadbare Poets* (1608).

LEMAN, "as tender as a parson's leman" (26*c*), mistress, concubine : also a gallant or lover. "They founde greater gaines by priestes lemmans then they were like to haue by priestes wives."—T. Wilson, *Rhet.* (1553), 28*b*.

LENGTH, "yourself to length it taketh direct trade" (14*c*), prolong, lengthen, spin out. "Thought must length it."—Daniel, *Zethys Festiv.* (1610), F. 3*b*.

LESE (24*c*, 39*b*, 51*b*, 67*c*, *et passim*), lose.

LESS, "who will do less than they that may do most" (39*d*).

LIES, "lies laid on by load" (78*d*).

LIFE, "what is life where living is extinct clear?" (90*c*).

LIGHT, (*a*) "light come, light go" (93*c*). "Wyte thou wele it schall be so, That lyghtly cum schall lyghtly go."—*Debate of the Carpenter's Tools.*
   (*b*) "light gains make heavy purses" (37*b*).
   (*c*) "ye stand in your own light" (62*c*), injure your own interests. "Take counsel and do not stand in your own light."—Jonson, *Tale of a Tub* (1633), ii. 1.

LIKE, "like will to like" (11*a*), a typical proverbial formula, with many variants—"like master, like man"; "like lord, like chaplain"; "like carpenter, like chips"; "like men, like manners," &c.: Fulwell's *Like Will to Like* is the title of an early play.

LIME-FINGERED (26*c*), given to pilfering. "They are light-footed and lime-fingered."—Purchas, *Pilgrimage* (1613), VIII. iv. 629.

LINE, (*a*) "as right as a line" (33*d*), in a direct course, straightforwardly, immediately : also line-right. "Streyt as lyne he com."—Chaucer, *Troilus* (*c.* 1374), II. 1412 (1461).
   (*b*) "we drew both in one line" (80*b*), were unanimous, in complete accord. "The Senat thus drawing all in a line."—Holland, *Livy* (1600), XLII. xxi. 1127.

LION, "as fierce as a lion of Cotsolde" (44*d*), a sheep : cf. *Essex* (or *Rumford*) *lion*=a calf. "Carlus is as

furious as a lyon of Cotsold."—Davies, *Epigrams*
(1596). "You stale old ruffian, you lion of Cotsolde."—*Sir John Oldcastle.*

LIPS, (*a*) " such lips, such lettice " (80*d*), see Like.
(*b*) " your lips hang in your light " (62*b*), *i.e.* hanging your lips in vexation is against your interests.

LIST, " which we list " (8*a*), like, wish, desire.

LISTENING, " I have learned in listening " (43*b*), cf.
" listeners hear no good of themselves."

LITHER, " too lither " (48*a*; also 73*c*), bad, rascally
inclined.

LITTER, " the litter is like to the sire and the dam "
(33*c*), see Like.

LOGIC, " she choppeth logic " (64*b*), argues a point, is
contentious, answers sharply. " If he heare you thus
play choploge."—Udall, *Roister Doister* (E.E.D.S.),
iii. 2.

LONG, " long be thy legs and short be thy life " (82*d*).

LONGETH, " that longeth thereto " (34*d*), is appropriate
to, that pertains to; often written " 'longeth," as if
=" belong." " With such austerity as longeth to a
father."—Shakspeare, *Taming of a Shrew* (1596),
iv. 4. 6.

LOOK, (*a*) " look ere thou leap " (7*c*), see Leap.
(*b*) " look as ye list " (91*c*), *list*=like, wish, desire.

LORD, (*a*) " there is no good accord where every man
would be a lord " (74*d*).
(*b*) " there is nothing in this world that agreeth
worse than doth a lord's heart and a beggar's purse "
(*Epigrams*), see Lady.

LORNE, " the corn is lorne " (27*d*), injured, ruined,
spoilt.

LOSE, " lose both living and love of all their kin "
(25*d*).

LOSERS, " let the losers have their words " (76*b*).

LOST, (*a*) " as good lost as found " (28*a*).
(*b*) " it is lost that is unsought " (38*c*).
(*c*) " like one half lost till greedy grasping got it "
(97*d*).

LOTHE, " the lothe stake " (60*d*), ugly, rough, misshapen.

LOVE, (*a*) " in love is no lack " (10*d*).

(*b*) " love me, love my dog " (93*a*), a proverb in the time of Saint Bernard. " *Cudora*. Love me?— love my dog! *Tharsalis*. I am bound to that by the proverb, madam."—Chapman, *Widow's Tears* (1612).

(*c*) " love me little, love me long " (57*b*). " *Bellamira*. Come, gentle Ithamore, lie in my lap. *Ithamore*. Love me little, love me long; let music rumble, Whilst I in thy incony lap do tumble."—Marlowe, *Jew of Malta* (1586), iv.

(*d*) " by love, without regard of living, these twain have wrought each other ill chieving " (48*c*).

(*e*) " love hath lost them the love of their friends " (48*d*).

(*f*) " we could live by love " (10*c*).

(*g*) " lovers live by love . . . as larks live by leeks " (25*c*).

(*h*) " what need we lump out love at once lashing " (57*a*).

LOVEDAY, " break a loveday " (69*b*), an agreement for the amicable settlement of a dispute. " He is more redy to make a fraye than a loue day."—Horman, *Vulg.* (1519), vii. 66 b.

MACKABROINE, " such a mackabroine " (74*c*), old hag: from Fr. *machabree*; Murray marks it " rare," and gives only the present instance.

MAISTER, " maister promotion saieth " (13*a*), master.

MAISTRY, " use maketh maistry " (55*d*), gives power, skill, the knowledge and experience which constitutes a master.

MAKE, (*a*) " make or mar I will " (*Epigrams*).

(*b*) " how flek and his make " (70*a*), *make*=companion. " This is no season To seek new makes in." —Jonson, *Tale of a Tub* (1633), i. 1.

MAKEBATE (24*a*), breeder of strife. " Such a malicious makebate."—More, *Suppl. Soulys* (1529), *Wks.*, 296. 2.

MALKIN, " more maids but Malkin " (32*c*), *Malkin* (=Mary) is generic for a woman of low birth, country wench, servant: frequently used proverbially to signify

drab, wanton. " There are more houses then Parishe
Churches, more maydes than Maulkin."—Gosson,
Sch. of Abuses (1597), 37 (Arber).

MALT, (*a*) " soft fire maketh sweet malt " (6*c*), an ad-
monition to be gentle or merciful : see Fire.

(*b*) " malt is above wheat with him " (31*a*), *i.e.*
" he is under the influence of drink." " Malt is now
aboue wheat with a number of mad people."—Breton,
Fantastickes (1626), B3.

MAN, see Play.

MARCH HARE, " as mad as a March hare " (73*a*), see
Hare.

MARE, (*a*) " my old mare would have a new crupper "
(52*d*).

(*b*) " the grey mare is the better horse " (64*a*), see
Horse.

(*c*) " well nigh every day a new mare or a moil "
(81*a*), *mare*=a woman (contemptuously) ; *moil*=mule
(also contemptuously of a trull, for the sake of the
rhyme).

MARKET, " the market goeth by the market men " (38*a*),
i.e. prices, rate of purchase and sale.

MARKS, " yet have ye other marks to rove at hand "
(37*a*), *rove*=to shoot at.

MARRIAGE, " a goodly marriage she is . . . were the
woman away " (52*d*), *i.e.* her money is desirable if
her person is not.

MARRY, " when men will needs marry wisdom and haste
may vary " (49*a*).

MARRYING, " marrying or marring " (18*c*), in slightly
different guise still proverbial.

MARYBONES, " on your marybones crouch to the ground "
(22*a*), the knees. " Down he fel vpon his maribones."
—More, *Confut. Tindale* (1532), *Wks.*, 727/2.

MASTERY, see Maistry.

MATINS, " if it be morn we have a pair of matins "
(78*a*).

MAUGRE, " maugre her head " (48*a*), in spite of : Fr.,
malgré.

MAY, (a) " that one may not another may " (55d).

(b) " he that will not when he may, when he would he shall have nay " (8a), also in Burton, *Melanch.* (1621).

MEALMOUTH (23d), a person of soft, carneying words, of hypocritical delicacy of speech : now surviving in " mealy-mouthed."

MEALS, " better are meals many than one too merry " (84a).

MEASURE, (a) " measure is a merry mean " (82a), moderation " *Magn.* Yet mesure is a mery mene. *Fan.* Yea, syr, a blannched almonde is no bene, Measure is mete for a marchauntes hall."—*Magnyfycence* (c. 1520). " There is measure in everything." —Shakspeare, *Much Ado* (1600), ii. 1.

(b) " thou fearest false measures " (*Epigrams*).

MEAT, (a) " look not on the meat but look on the man " (62a).

(b) " that one loveth not, another doth, which hath sped All meats to be eaten and all maids to be wed " (55d).

MEDDLING, " of little meddling cometh great rest " (57d). " Grete reste stande in lytell besynesse, Beware also to sporne against a wall."—Lydgate, *Proverbes.*

MEET-MATE (42c), helpmate : cf. *meet-help* = help-meet, a wife. " In my discoveries of him and his meet-help." —Spratt, *Relation of Young's Contrivance.*

MELANCHOLY, " turn melancholy to mirth " (88d).

MEND, (a) " if every man mend one, all shall be mended " (*Epigrams*), many hands make light work.

(b) " I will mend this house and pair another " (88d), *pair* = impair, neglect. " He bulde newe citees and amended citees þat were i-peyred."—Trevisa, *Higden* (Rolls), vi. 399 (1387).

MERCHANT, (a) " ye merchant " (31c ; also 66c), a familiar address—" fellow," " chap." " I would have so scourged my marchant, that his breech should ake." —*New Custom* (c. 1550), *Anon. Plays* (E.E.D.S.), Ser. 3, 162b.

(b) " a merchant without either money or ware " (66c).

MERRIER, " the more the merrier " (79c). " Store makes no sore : loe this seemes contrarye, And mo the merier is a Proverbe eke, But store of sores maye make a maladye, And one to many maketh some to seeke, When two be mette that bankette with a leche."—Gaiscoigne, *Posies* (1575).

MERRY, (a) " good to be merry and wise " (6d). " I . . . garnished my shop, for want of plate, with good wholesome, thriftie sentences ; as, ' Touchstone, keepe thy shoppe, and thy shoppe will keepe thee.' ' Light gaines make heavie purses.' ' Tis good to be merry and wise.' "—*Eastward Hoe* (1605).

(b) " merry as a cricket " (31b)—" merry as a pie " (60a). " By the Lord of Ludgate, my Liege, I'll be as merrie as a Pie."—Decker, *Shomakers Holiday* (1600).

(c) " it is merry in hall when beards wag all " (79d), see Hall. " Swithe mury hit is in halle When burdes wawen alle."—*Life of Alexander* (1312). " Be merry, be merry, my wife has all ; For women are shrews, both short and tall, 'Tis merry in hall when beards wag all."—Shakspeare, 2 *Henry IV.* (1598), v. 3.

MESS, " to keep yet one mess . . . in store " (89b), " put by something for a rainy day."

MESSENGER, " to come . . . before the messenger " (31c), to be " previous," be one's own postman.

MEVE (15c, 59b, 84d, *et passim*), move.

MEW, " hawks in the mew " (66b), properly a cage for hawks : figuratively a place where anything is in keeping.

MIGHT, " might overcometh right " (69a), in modern phrase, " might is right."

MILK, " milk is white, And lieth not in the dike, But all men know it good meal " (62d).

MILL, " much water goeth by the mill that the miller knoweth not of " (73d). " What, man ; more water glideth by the mill, Than wots the miller of, and easy it is Of a cut loaf to steal a shive."—Shakspeare, *Titus Andronicus* (1593), ii. 7.

MILLSTONE, " she had seen far in a millstone " (25*d*) :
" to look (or see) into a millstone "=to fathom a
secret; to be far or sharp sighted. " Your eies are
so sharp that you cannot onely looke through a mil-
stone, but cleane through the minde, and so cunning
that you can levell at the dispositions of women whom
you never knew."—Lyly, *Euphues and his England.*

MINION (40*b*), " a creature " : here a debased sense of
minion=favourite; *i.e.* an unworthy or unseemly
favourite.

MINISH, MINISHETH (99*a*, 76*a*), diminish. " To abbridge
his power, and to minishe his authoritie."—Hall,
Henry VI. f. 81.

MIRE, " lay my credence in the mire " (57*d*), compare
" to drag one's reputation through the mud."

MISERY, " misery may be mother where one beggar is
driven to beg of another " (100*a*).

MISRECKONING, " misreckoning is no payment " (64*d*).

MO (12*c*, 19*a*), more.

MOCK, " he mocked much of her " (53*c*), feigned, pre-
tended to make. " He mocks the pauses that he
makes."—Shakspeare, *Antony and Cleopatra* (1608),
v. 1.

MOCKAGE, " half in mockage " (25*c*), mocking. " But
all this perchaunce ye were I speake half in moccage."
—Sir Thos. Chaloner, *Moriæ Enc.* (1549), M 3.

MOLT, " my heart for woe molt " (91*a*), melted : an old
form.

MONK, " like a bean in a monk's hood " (76*c*), *i.e.* lost,
like a nonentity : *bean*=a low standard of value.

MONTH, " better is one month's cheer than a churl's
whole life " (84*a*) : cf. Tennyson's " better fifty years
of Europe than a cycle of Cathay."

MOON, (*a*) " to cast beyond the moon " (11*c*), to calcu-
late deeply ; make an extravagant conjecture ; be ambi-
tious ; to attempt impossibilities. " But oh, I talk
of things impossible And cast beyond the moon."—
T. Heywood, *A Woman Kill'd with Kindness*
(*c.* 1603).

HEY. PROV.   N

(*b*) " to make me believe . . . that the moon is made of a green cheese " (84*d*), to hoax, quiz, " chaff." " Whilst they tell for truthe Luther his lowde lyes, so that they may make theyr blinde brotherhode and the ignorant sort beleve that the mone is made of grene chese."—Shacklock, *Hatchet of Heresies* (1565).

MOONSHINE, " moonshine in the water " (44*c*), an illusive shadow.

MORE, " for little more or less no debate make " (68*d*), trouble not about trifles ; seek not to enforce a difference between Tweedledum and Tweedledee.

MORNINGS, " cloudy mornings turn to clear afternoons " (98*c*).

MOSS, see Rolling stone.

MOTE, " ye can see a mote in another man's eye, but ye cannot see a baulk in your own " (81*c*), *baulk*= beam, rafter.

MOTHER, " your mother bid till ye were born " (98*a*).

MOUSE, (*a*) " as sure as a mouse tied with a thread " (86*c*).
(*b*) " a mouse in time may bite in two a cable " (82*b*).
(*c*) " it had need to be a wily mouse that should breed in the cat's ear " (71*d*).

MOUTH, (*a*) " that shall not stop my mouth " (64*c*), *i.e.* silence me.
(*b*) " to make up my mouth " (43*c*), *i.e.* to give cause for arranging the features to produce a particular expression ; cf. " make up a face," " make up a lip," &c. ; thus to induce a grimace or wry face : now American by survival. " Make up your face [to a weeping person] quickly."—Brome, *Jovial Crew* (1641), iv. 1.
(*c*) " ye speak now as ye would creep into my mouth " (94*c*).
(*d*) " till meat fall in your mouth will ye lie in bed " (21*c*).

MUCH, see Made.

MUCK, " muck of the world " (44*c*), money. " For to pinche, and for to spare, Of worlds mucke to gette encres."—Gower, *Confessio Amantis*, v.

MUM, " I will say nought but mum, and mum is coun‧ sel " (65b), *mum*=a warning to silence.

MUSCLES, " as handsomely as a bear picketh muscles " (66a).

MUSTARD, " he will kill a man for a mess of mustard " (*Epigrams*).

NAIL, (a) " one nail driveth out another " (*Epigrams*).
(b) " this hitteth the nail on the head " (101d), to get at the bottom of a matter, to succeed, to come to the point. In *Sir Thomas More* (c. 1590), " my lord Cardinal's players, in answer to the question as to what pieces compose their repertory, reply :—Divers, my Lord, *The Cradle of Security, Hit Nail o' th' Head, Impatient Poverty, The Play of Four P's, Dives and Lazarus, Lusty Juventus,* and the *Marriage of Wit and Wisdom.*"

NAY, (a) " say nay and take it " (*Epigrams*) : another version is, " Maids say ' No ' and mean ' Yes.' "
(b) " ye may mend three nays with one yea " (35d).

NE (*passim*), not, nor : frequently in M.E. joined with the verbs " to have," " to be," and " to will " : thus, *nam*=*ne am*=am not, *nis*=is not, *nill*=*ne will*=will not, *nadde*=*ne hadde*=had not, &c.

NEAR, " near is my smock " (28d), nearer. " Of friends, of foes, behold my foule expence, And never the neere."—*Mirror for Mag.* (1559), 364.

NEED, (a) " need hath no law " (25b and *Epigrams*), in modern phrase : " Needs must where the devil drives."
(b) " need maketh the old wife trot " (99d), Fr., " besoin fait vieille trotter " (Roman de Trubert, c. 1300).

NET, " the rough net is not the best catcher of birds " (22b).

NETTLE, " she had pist on a nettle " (99c), was peevish, out of temper.

NEW MAN, " showing himself a new man " (89c), through having reformed.

NEWER, " newer is truer " (63a).

NOBLES, "a bag of . . . nobles" (97*a*), *noble* = a gold coin struck by Edward III., and originally of the value of 6s. 8d. In the reigns of Henry VI. and Edward IV., the value of the noble having risen to 10s., another gold coin of the same value as the original noble was issued called an angel (*q.v.*). Half-nobles and quarter-nobles were also current.

NOON, (*a*) "go to bed at noon" (85*a*), betimes, unconscionably early.

(*b*) "the longer forenoon the shorter afternoon" (50*b*).

NOPPY, "some noppy ale" (45*b*), usually *nappy* = strong, "heady." "Nappy liquor will lullaby thy fine wittes."—*New Letter* (1593).

NOSE, (*a*) "thou canst hold my nose to the grindstone" (13*b* and *Epigrams*), oppress, harass, punish, hold at a disadvantage. "A shame and . . . vilanie for you . . . hable to hold their nose to the grindstone, nowe . . . to be their pezantes, whose lordes your aunccettors were."—Aylmer, Harborough, &c., 1559 (*Maitland on Ref.*, 220). "They might be ashamed, for lack of courage, to suffer the Lacedæmonians to hold their noses to the grindstone."—North, *Plutarch* (1578), 241.

(*b*) "your nose drops . . . I will eat no browesse sops" (87*d*), *brose* in O.E. = bread and fat meat (Huloet). "That tendre browyce made with a maryboon."—Lydgate, *Order of Fooles* (d. 1460).

(*c*) [I shall] "wipe your nose upon your sleeve" (97*c*), affront. "There is one Sophos, a brave gentleman; he'll wipe your son Peter's nose of Mistress Lelia."—*Wily Beguiled* (1606) [Dodsley, *Old Plays* (1874), ix. 242].

(*d*) see Pepper.

NOTHER (*passim*), neither.

NOTHING, (*a*) "nothing hath no savour" (20*b*), *i.e.* there is no savour in want.

(*b*) "where as nothing is the king must lose his right" (47*d*), *i.e.* even the king can get nothing from nothing.

(*c*) "where nothing is a little thing doth ease" (29*b*).

NOUGHT, (a) " nought venture, nought have " (38c).
  (b) " nought lay down, nought take up " (41c).
  (c) " a thing of nought " (43c).
  (d) " whom I made of nought " (65c)—" bring to nought " (65d).

NUN, " as nice as a nun's hen " (52c), see Hen.

NURSE, " God send that head a better nurse " (85d).

NUT, " knack me that nut " (80c), solve me that problem, explain that, overcome this difficulty : *knack* =crack.

NYCEBECETUR, " your ginifinee nycebecetur " (32d), apparently a term of contempt : Heywood uses it again in *Play of the Mather* (E.E.D.S., *Works*, I. 123), " such nycebyceturs as she is." The word has puzzled all editors so far ; all that seems clear is that Heywood in each case employs the word in contempt of a woman, as also does Udall. " *Merygreeke*. But with whome is he nowe so sadly roundyng yond? *Doughtie*. With Nobs nicebecetur miserere fonde."—*Roister Doister*, I. iv. 12. A somewhat exhaustive enquiry on the phrase is summed up in Heywood's *Works* (E.E.D.S.), III. Notebook *s.v.* Nicebecetur.

OAR, " she (or he) must have an oar in every man's barge " (24b), meddle in the business or affairs of others : somewhat earlier, the proverb occurs in a ballad entitled " Long have I bene a singing man," by John Redford (c. 1540). " In each mannes bote would he have an ore."—Udall, *Eras. Apop.* (c. 1543), II. 180.

ONY, " had I ony " (96b), any.

OR (*passim*), ere, before, lest, than.

OSTE, " ye would now here oste " (34c), dwell, remain : *i.e.* Host.

O'THING, " this o'thing " (29c), one thing : O=numeral adjective, a reduced form of ôn, oon : cf. nothing. " O flessh they been, and o flessh as I gesse Hath but oon herte, in wele and in distresse."—Chaucer, *Merch. T.* (c. 1386), 91. " Ill huswiferie othing or other must craue."—Tusser, *Husb.* (1573), 184 (1878).

OUT, " out of sight, out of mind " (8*d*).

OUT ILES (41*d*), properly islands away from the mainland : here figuratively for an outlandish district, up-country away from a centre of population.

OVEN, " no man will another in the oven seek, except that himself have been there before " (84*b*), the commonest version is, " no woman will her daughter seek in the oven," &c. " A hackney proverb in men's mouths ever since King Lud was a little boy, or Belinus, Brennus' brother, for the love hee bare to oysters, built Billingsgate."—Nash, *Have with you to Saffron Waldon* (1596), 157.

OVERTHWART, " overthwart the shins " (24*c*), across.

OWL, " keep corners, or hollow trees with th' owl " (71*c*).

OWN, " alway own is own at the reckoning's end " (64*d*).

PAD, " it will breed a pad in the straw " (63*d*), a lurking or hidden danger. " Though they make never so fayre a face, yet there is a padde in the strawe."—Palsgrave, &c. (1530), 595, 1.

PAIN, (*a*) " change from ill pain to worse is worth small hire " (72*c*).
    (*b*) " plant your own pain " (69*b*).
    (*c*) " I have wrought mine own pain " (26*a*).
    (*d*) " take a pain for a pleasure all wise men can " (13*d*).

PAIR, see Mend.

PANNIER, see Pig.

PARING, " she will not part with the paring of her nails " (40*a*).

PARISH PRIEST, " the parish priest forgetteth that ever he hath been holy water clerk " (38*b*).

PARS VERS, " tell him he's pars vers " (59*c*), perverse.

PARSONS, " long standing and small offering maketh poor parsons " (98*a*).

PAST, " let all things past, pass " (90*b*), let bygones be bygones ; let sleeping dogs lie.

PATERNOSTER, (a) " he may be in my paternoster . . .
but . . . he shall never come in my creed " (96c).
" I trust yee remember your jugling at Newington
with a christall stone, your knaveries in the wood by
Wanstead, the wondrous treasure you would discover
in the Isle of Wight, al your villanies about that
peece of service, as perfectly known to some of my
friends yet living as their Paster-noster, who curse the
time you ever came into their creed."—Chettle, *Kind-
Heart's Dream* (1592).

(b) " no penny, no paternoster " (96c), no pay, no
prayers. " The Pater-noster, which was wont to fill
a sheet of paper, is written in the compasse of a
penny ; whereupon one merrily assumed that proverbe
to be derived, No penny no pater-noster. Which their
nice curtayling putteth mee in minde of the custome
of the Scythians, who, if they had beene at any time
distressed with famine, tooke in their girdles shorter."
—Greene, *Arcadia* (1587).

(c) " pattering the devil's paternoster to himself "
(39b), grumbling, muttering imprecations. " Yet wol
they seyn harm and grucche and murmure priuely for
verray despit, whiche wordes men clepen the deueles
Pater noster."—Chaucer, *Pars. T.* (c. 1386), 434.

PATIENCE, " let patience grow in your garden alway "
(44d).

PAY, see Shot.

PAYMENT, " misreckoning is no payment " (64d).

PEAS, " who hath many peas may put the more in the
pot " (12c).

PENNY, (a) " a penny for your thought " (61b), a call to
persons in a " brown study." " Come, friar, I will
shake him from his dumps. How cheer you, sir? a
penny for your thought."—Greene, *Friar Bacon* (1588),
161.

(b) " to turn the penny " (92b), earn money : the
phrase occurs (1510) in Foxe's *Acts and Monuments*,
iv. " His wyfe made hym so wyse, That he wolde
tourne a peny twyse, And then he called it a
ferthynge."—*Maid Emlyn* (c. 1520) [Hazlitt, *Early
Pop. Poet.* iv. 85].

(c) " not one penny to bless him " (89a), very poor.

PEPPER, (a) "pepper in the nose" (64c), quick at offence, testy : Fr., *moutarde au nez*. "There are ful proude-herted men paciente of tonge, And boxome as of berynge to burgeys and to lordes, And to pore peple hav peper in the nose."—Langland, *Piers Plowman* (1362), xv. 197.

(b) "pepper is black and hath a good smack" (62d).

PETER, "to rob Peter and pay Paul" (31c), to take of one to give to another. The proverb pretty certainly derives its origin from the fact that in the reign of Edward VI. the lands of St. Peter at Westminster were appropriated to raise money for the repair of St. Paul's in London. John Thirlby, the first and only Bishop of Westminster (1541-50), "having wasted the patrimony allotted by the King (Hen. VIII.) for the support of the see, was translated to Norwich, and with him ended the bishopric of Westminster" (Haydn, *Dignities*). Heylin (*Hist. Ref.* i. 256, 1661) says that the lands at Westminster were so dilapidated by Bishop Thirlby that there was almost nothing to support the dignity. . . . Most of the lands invaded by the great men of the Court, the rest laid out for reparation to the Church of St. Paul, pared almost to the very quick in those days of rapine. From hence, he says, came first that significant byword (as is said by some) of robbing Peter to pay Paul. The French form of the proverb, "découvrir saint Pierre pour couvrir saint Paul" gives additional colouring to the statement, and is supported by Barclay in his *Eclogues* (Percy Soc. xxiii. xvii.), "They robbe St. Peter to cloth St. Paul."

PICKTHANK (23d), toady : also as verb. "There be two tythes, rude and ranke, Symkyn Tytyuell and Pers Pykthanke."—Skelton, *Works* (1513-25), ii. 60 (Dyce).

PIE, "merry as a pie" (60a).

PIECE, "this maid, the piece peerless in mine eye" (10c), *piece*=a person, male or female : often in contempt. "His princess say you? . . . Ay, the most peerless piece."—Shakspeare, *Winter's Tale* (1604), v. 1.

PIG, (a) " a pig of mine own sow " (78c).

(b) " to buy the pig in the poke " (97d), of a blind bargain. " And in the floor, with nose and mouth to broke, They walwe as doon two pigges in a poke."— Chaucer, *Reeves Tale* (c. 1386), 358.

(c) " yet snatch ye at the poke that the pig is in, not for the poke, but the pig good cheap to win " (97d).

(d) " when the pig is proffered . . . hold up the poke " (8c), " never refuse a good bargain." " When me profereth the pigge, open the poghe."—*Douce MS.* (c. 1400), 52.

(e) " bid me welcome, pig ; I pray thee kiss me " (79d).

(f) " a pig of the worse panier " (102c).

PIKE, " one good lesson . . . I pike " (8c, 11a, 72b), mark, note, learn, pick out.

PIKED, " a pretty piked matter " (44c), *piked* = marked : thus " a pretty kettle of fish."

PILATE'S VOICE (25a), a loud, ranting voice. " In Pilate voys he gan to cry, And swor by armes, and by blood and bones."—Chaucer, *Cant. Tales* (c. 1386), 3126.

PINCHPENNY, " that benchwhistler is a pinchpenny " (37c), a niggard in food, dress, or money : it early occurs in Occleve (1412), *De Reg. Princip.* " They accompt one . . . a pynch penny if he be not prodygall."—Lyly, *Euphues, Anat. of Wit* (1579), 109.

PIPE, (a) " who that leaveth surety and leaneth unto chance when fools pipe, by authority he may dance " (101d).

(b) " to dance after her pipe " (75b).

(c) " he can ill pipe that lacketh his upper lip " (94c).

PITCHERS, " small pitchers have wide ears " (65c), usually of children : what children hear at home soon flies abroad. " *Q. Elizabeth.* A parlous boy ; go to, you are too shrewd. *Archbishop.* Good madam, be not angry with the child. *Q. Elizabeth.* Pitchers have ears."—Shakspeare, *Richard III.* (1597), ii. 4.

PLAIN, " plain without pleats " (69b), in the *Epigrams on Proverbs* (201) it is thus amplified, " the plain fashion is best . . . plain without plates."

PLAY, " as good play for nought as work for nought "
(44*b*).

PLEASURE, (*a*) " who will in time present, pleasure refrain, shall in time to come more pleasure obtain "
(32*d*).

   (*b*) " flee pleasure and pleasure will follow thee:
follow pleasure and then will pleasure flee " (32*d*).

PLENTY, " plenty is no dainty " (62*b*).

POMPOUS PROVISION, " pompous provision cometh not all
alway of gluttony but of pride some time " (81*d*).

POST, (*a*) " from post to pillar I have been tost " (55*c*),
hither and thither, with aimless effort or action:
literally, from the same to the same—*pillar* = Lat.
columna = *post*. Thus in the *Ayenbite of Inwit* a
good man becomes a post in God's temple. " And,
dainty duke, whose doughty dismal fame From Dis
to Dædalus, from post to pillar, Is blown abroad."—
Shakspeare and Fletcher, *Two Noble Kinsmen* (*c.*
1611), iii. 5.

   (*b*) " in post pace " (51*b*), with all possible speed
or expedition. " Lord George your brother, Norfolk,
and myself, In haste, post-haste, are come to join with
you."—Shakspeare, 3 *Henry VI.* (1594), ii. 1.

   (*c*) " a mill post thwitten to a pudding prick "
(101*a*), said of unthrifts: *twitten* = to whittle down;
pudding prick = the skewer used to fasten a pudding
bag.

   (*d*) " a post of physic " (55*c*), probably a posset.

POT, (*a*) " the weaker goeth to the pot " (68*d*), *pot* has
been thought to = (*a*) pit (*i.e.* of destruction), or (*b*)
the melting pot of the refiner: the meaning, however,
is clear, and the colloquialism, though ancient, is still
in common use. In the illustration (*infra*) and in
many monkish references the " pit " or " pot " is
obviously a kind of oubliette, in which refractory
monks or impenitent heretics were immured, suffering
a lingering or speedy death at the will of their
gaolers. " Under a pot he schal be put in a pryvie
chamber."—*Piers Plowman*, 62.

   (*b*) "the pot so long to the water goeth, till at the
last it cometh home broken " (82*b*), *i.e.* the inevitable
must happen. " So long went the pot to the water,

that at last it came broken home, and so long put he his hand into his purse, that at last the empty bottome returned him a writ of *Non est inventus.*"—Greene, *Never too Late* (1590).

(c) " neither pot broken nor water spilt."

(d) " to see the pot both skimmed for running over and also all the liquor run at rover " (99b), *to run at rover*=to have too much liberty : here=squandered, dissipated.

(e) " he that cometh last to the pot is soonest wroth " (99b).

(f) " my pot is whole and my water is clean " (83a).

(g) " little pot soon hot " (31b), a little suffices; little people (or minds) are soon angered. " Now were I not a little pot, and soon hot, my very lips might freeze to my very teeth, . . . for, considering the weather, a taller man than I will take cold."—Shakspeare, *Taming of the Shrew* (1593), iv. 1.

POTTED, " she was potted thus like a sot " (99b), ruined : see Pot (a).

POVERTY, " poverty parteth fellowship " (48d).

PERIL, " the peril of prating out of tune by note " (68c).

PRAYERS, " much motion . . . to prayers with . . . little devotion " (96c).

PREASE, " some folk in luck cannot prease " (21b, 34c), press forward, hasten, " crowd in." " No humble suitors prease to speak for right."—Shakspeare, 3 *Henry VI.* (1595), iii. 1.

PREFE (in pl. PREVES), " some case . . . showeth prefe " (46d, 27d), proof.

PRICK, (a) " folly it is to spurn against a prick " (68b), in Biblical phrase, " to kick against," &c.

(b) " ye shoot nigh the prick " (15a), in archery the point or mark in the centre of the butts ; or, as we should now say, " the bull's-eye." " Therefore seeing that which is most perfect and best in shootinge, as alwayes to hit the pricke, was never seene nor hard tell on yet amonges men."—Ascham, *Toxoph.* (1544), 123.

PRIDE, (a) " pride will have a fall " (27a).
(b) " pride goeth before and shame cometh after "
(27b). " Pryde gothe before and shame cometh be-
hynde . . . We may wayle the tyme that ever it
came here."—*Treatise of a Gallant* (c. 1510).

PRIEST, " I would do more than the priest spake of on
Sunday " (95d).

PROFACE (79b), " much good may it do you ! " a common
welcome at meals : in the *Epigrams* we have, " Reader
. . . for preface, proface." " The dinner's half done
before I say grace, And bid the old knight and his
guest proface."—Heywood, *Wise Wom. of Hogsdon*
(1638).

PROFFERED, " proffered service stinketh " (61a).

PROPERTY, " her property preves " (27d), cloak, disguise.

PROPHET, " not to my profit a prophet was I " (91b),
the pun still does yeoman service as such.

PROUD, " I proud and thou proud who shall bear th'
ashes out ? " (26d).

PROVENDER, " his provender pricketh him " (*Epigrams*).

PUDDING TIME, " this year cometh . . . in pudding
time " (97c), in the nick of time, opportunely. " You
come in pudding time, or else I had dress'd them."—
Tylney, *Locrine* (1594), iii. 3.

PULPIT, " a proper pulpit piece " (82c), " gospel," something to be received without question because ex-
pounded as it were *ex cathedrâ*.

PURSE, (a) " the purse is threadbare " (20b).
(b) " he is purse sick and lacketh a physician "
(41b), needy, hard up.
(c) " ye would by my purse give me a purgation "
(41a).
(d) " be it better, be it worse, love ye after him
that beareth the purse " (13a).

PUT, see Case.

QUEANS, " flearing queans " (66a), wantons, strumpets :
primarily *quean* (like queen)=a woman without regard
to character or position ; the spelling ultimately differ-

entiated the debased from the reputable meaning, a
noteworthy instance occurring in Langland (*Piers
Plowman* [1363], ix. 46, " At church in the charnel
cheorles aren yuel to knowe Other a knyght fro a
knave other a queyne fro a queene."

QUESTION, " this is a question of old enquiring " (91*a*).

QUIGHT (47*d*), quit.

RABBIT, " like the devil will change a rabbit for a rat "
(86*a*).

RATE, " rise ye as ye rate " (55*d*), reckon, fix, decide.

RAVINE, " ruin of one ravine " (93*c*), *ravine*=an act of
rapine. " I sorowed for the provinces misfortunes,
wrackt by private ravins and publick taxes."—Q. Eliz.
tr. *Boeth.* (1593), I. pr. iv. 9.

RECEIVERS, " where be no receivers, there be no thieves "
(48*c*). " And it is a comon sayinge, ware there no
receyver there shoulde be no thefe. So ware there no
stewes, there shulde not so many honeste mennes
doughters rune awaye from there fathers and playe the
whores as dothe."—*A Christen Exhortation unto
Customable Swearers* (1575).

RECKONERS, (*a*) " reckoners without their host must
reckon twice " (19*d*). Fr., " Comptoit sans son hoste."
—Rabelais, *Gargantua.*
(*b*) " even reckoning maketh long friends " (64*d*).

RECUMBENTIBUS (85*b*), a knock-down blow : cf. " circum-
bendibus." " He yaff the Kyng Episcropus 'Suche a
recumbentibus, He smot in-two bothe helme and
mayle."—*Laud Troy Bk.* (*c.* 1400), 7400.

RELEVAVITH, " what shall be his relevavith " (36*a*),
relief. " I see not any greate lightlywod that any
good summe will comm in, tyl after Christmas, and
then no more than the releuauithes."—*State Papers,
Hen. VIII.* (1546), I. ii. 840.

RESTY, " resty wealth " (12*d*): *resty* may be subject to
three glosses=(*a*) indolent, lazy : meaning that wealth
obtained by a rich marriage tends thereto ; or (*b*) it
may=restive, coy (as hard to get) ; or (*c*)=it may be
a contemptuous application of *resty*=rancid, thus

referring to money as " dross," " muck," &c. " Where
the master is too resty or too rich to say his own
prayers, or to bless his own table."—Milton, *Icono-
clastes* (1649), xxiv.

REWETH (78*c*), rues.

RICHES, " riches bringeth oft harm and ever fear, where
poverty passeth without grudge of grief " (46*d*).

RICHESSE, " beauty without richesse " (14*b*), riches:
properly a singular, but now used as a plural.

RID, see Rock.

RIGHT SIDE, " you rose on your right side " (62*c*), a
happy augury : the modern usage speaks of the reverse
or " wrong side of the bed." " *C*. What ! doth shee
keepe house alreadie? *D*. Alreadie. *C*. O good God :
we rose on the right side to-day."—*Terence in English*
(1614).

RIME, " it may rime but it accordeth not " (44*c*). " It
may wele ryme but it accordith nought."—Lydgate,
MS. poem, " On Inconstancy."

RING, " I hopping without for a ring of a rush " (9*a*),
see Rush-ring.

RINGLEADER (24*d*), originally one who led a ring, as of
dancers, &c.

RIPE, " soon ripe soon rotten " (27*c*) : this proverb also
occurs in Harman, *Caveat,* &c. (1567).

ROAST, (*a*) " rule the roast " (13*a*), to have (or take)
the lead (or mastery) : *roast*=roost (probably). " But
at the pleasure of me That ruleth the roste alone."—
Skelton, *Colyn Cloute* (*c*. 1518).
  (*b*) " he looked like one that had beshit the roast "
(89*c*).
  (*c*) " roast a stone " (56*c*), *i.e.* one may put warmth
into but can never get heat out of a stone. " They may
garlicke pill Cary sackes to the mil Or pescoddes they
may shil Or els go roste a stone."—Skelton, *Why
come ye not to Court?* (1520).

ROBBERY, " change is no robbery " (*Epigrams*), see
Change.

ROBIN HOOD, " tales of Robin Hood are good among fools " (94c), the story of Robin Hood ultimately grew so misty and traditional that the name became a generic byword for the marvellous that was not believable. Thus Robin Hood, *subs.* = a daring lie; Robin Hood's pennyworth (of things sold under value); " Good even, good Robin Hood " (said of civility extorted by fear); " Many talk of Robin Hood that never shot in his bow " (75a) = many speak of things of which they have no knowledge; and " Tales of Robin Hood are good enough for fools." " I write no ieste ne tale of Robin Hood."—Barclay, *Ship of Fooles* (1509), fol. 250 (1570).

ROCK, " thus rid the rock " (92b and *Epigrams*), *i.e.* so was the distaff managed, manipulated : *rock* = the distaff or frame about which flax, wool, &c., was arranged and from which the thread was drawn in spinning. Hence here the meaning is " So managed you your thrift badly:" " I'll ride your horse as well as I ride you."—Shakspeare, *Twelfth Night* (1602), iii. 4.

ROD, (a) " when haste proveth a rod made for his own tail " (7a).
   (b) " beaten with his own rod " (7a). " —— don fust C'on kint sovent est-on batu."—*Roman du Renart* (c. 1300).

ROLLING STONE, " the rolling stone never gathereth moss " (31c). " I, thy head is alwaies working; it roles, and it roles, Dondolo, but it gathers no mosse, Dondolo."—Marston, *Fawn* (1606). " Pierre volage ne queult mousse."—*De l'Hermite qui se désespéra pour le Larron qui ala en Paradis avant que lui* (13th century).

ROME, " Rome was not built in one day and yet stood till it was finished " (36d). " Hæc tamen vulgaris sententia me aliquantulum recreavit, quæ etsi non auferre, tamen minuere possit dolorem meum, quæ quidem sententia hæc est, Romam uno die non fuisse conditam."—Queen Elizabeth, *Extempore speech before the University of Cambridge* (9th August, 1564).

ROOF, " he is at three words up in the house roof " (66d) : nowadays we say " up in the skies."

ROPE, (*a*) " as meet as a rope for a thief " (24*c*).
(*b*) " he hauleth her by the boy rope " (78*c*), see Boy rope.

ROUTING, " routing like a hog " (30*a*), *rout* = snore.

ROVERS, " ye pry and ye prowl at rovers " (31*c*)—" let not your tongue run at rover " (69*a*)—(also 99*b*), *at rover* = wild, unrestrained, at random.

ROYALS (*i.e.* RIAL), " a bag of royals and nobles " (97*a*), *royal* = an old English gold coin, of varying value, from 10s. in Henry VI.'s time to 15s. in Queen Elizabeth's, whilst in the reign of James I. the rose-rial was worth 30s., and the spur-rial, 15s. : see Noble.

ROYLE, " by your revellous riding on every royle " (81*a*). *royle* = a Flemish horse : this would seem to echo the alleged contempt of Henry VIII. as regards Anne of Cleves, whom he described as " a Flanders mare."

RUIN, " ruin of one ravin was there none greater " (73*c*), see Ravine.

RULE, " better to rule than be ruled by the rout " (13*a*).

RUN, (*a*) " he may ill run that cannot go " (94*b*).
(*b*) " ye run to work in haste as nine men held ye " (42*c*).
(*c*) " she thinketh I run over all that I look on " (77*c*), examine, " possess," have to do with.

RUNNETH, " he runneth far that never turneth again " (90*b*).

RUSH, " care not a rush " (95*a*), *rush* = low standard of value. " And yet yeve ye me nevere The worthe of a risshe."—Langland, *Piers Plowman* (1362), 2421.

RUSHES, " green rushes for this stranger, straw here " (59*b*) : it was usual, before the introduction of carpets, to strew rushes on the floors of dwelling-houses ; and on the entrance of a visitor, hospitality required that they should be renewed. " Where is this stranger? Rushes, ladies, rushes : Rushes as green as summer for this stranger."—Beaumont and Fletcher, *Valentinian* (1617), ii. 4.

RUSH-RING, " a ring of a rush " (9a), a *rush ring*=a symbol of a mock marriage. " As fit . . . as Tib's rush for Tom's forefinger."—Shakspeare, *All's Well* (1598), ii. 2, 22.

SACK, (a) " an old sack axeth much patching " (58a).
   (b) " it is a bad sack that will abide no clouting " (60d).

SADDLES, " where saddles lack better ride on a pad than on the horse bareback " (29b).

SAGE, " sage said saws " (7b).

SAID, (a) " sooner said than done " (73b).
   (b) " little said soon amended " (*Epigrams*), the modern form is " least said soonest mended."
   (c) " other folks said it but she did it " (99d).

SAINT, (a) " young saint, old devil " (27c), the reverse was quite as common—" young devil, old saint."

SAINT AUDRY (73d), or Auldrey, meaning Saint Etheldreda, who (by tradition) died of a swelling in her throat, which she considered as a particular judgment for having been in her youth much addicted to wearing fine necklaces (Nich. Harpsfield (1622), *Hist. Eccl. Anglicana*) : hence tawdry.

SAVOURLY, " very savourly sound " (14b), properly, rightly—as with a good and proper sense.

SAY, " I say little but I think more " (57b).

SAYING, (a) " saying and doing are two things " (73b).
   (b) " saying that ye never saw " (33a).

SCARBOROUGH WARNING, " Scarborough warning I had " (43b), *i.e.* no warning at all ; a blow before the word. Fuller in his *Worthies* says : " The proverb took its original from Thomas Stafford, who in the reign of Queen Mary, 1557, with a small company seized on Scarborough Castle (utterly destitute of provision for resistance) before the townsmen had the least notice of his approach." " I received a message from my lord chamberlaine . . . that I should preach before him upon Sunday next ; which Scarborough warning did not only perplex me, but so puzzel me."—Mayhew, *Letter* (1603, 19th January).

HEY. PROV.   O

SEE, (a) " see me and see me not " (69c).
   (b) " I see much, but I say little and do less " (41b).

SEEK, (a) " to seek for that she was loth to find " (71a)—
" I seek for a thing . . . that I would not find"
(*Epigrams*).

SEELED WHEN, " in coming seeled when " (44b), seldom.

SEEN, " seen of the tone sort and heard of the tother"
(101b).

SEGGING, " the Dutchman saith that segging is good
cope " (94a), *segging* = sedge.

SELDOM, (a) " seldom cometh the better " (11a). " This
change is like to the rest of worldly chaunges, that is,
from the better to the worse : For as the Proverb
sayth : Seldome coms the better."—*English Courtier
and Country Gentleman* (1586).
   (b) " seldom seen, soon forgotten " (30d).

SELF, " self do, self have " (20a).

SENIOR DE GRAUNDE (13a). " I myself will mounsire
graunde captain undertake."—Udall, *Roister Doister*
(E.E.D.S.), iv. 8, 98b.

SERVICE, " proffered service stinketh " (61a), see Proffered.

SHALL, " that shall be, shall be " (53b), the modern
" we shall see what we shall see " is regarded as an
echo of the Fr. *nous verrons que nous verrons,* whereas the idiom is of native growth.

SHAME, " shame take him that shame thinketh " (21b),
i.e. " Honi soit qui mal y pense."

SHAMEFUL, " shameful craving must have shameful
way " (35d).

SHARP, " all thing that is sharp is short " (56d).

SHEAF, " take as falleth in the sheaf " (64b).

SHEATH, " she maketh so much of her painted sheath "
(26d).

SHEEP, (a) " as rich as a new shorn sheep " (42d),
penniless, " fleeced." " The nexte that came was a
coryar And a Cobelar, his brother, As ryche as a new
shorne shepe."—*Cocke Lorelles Bote (c.* 1510).
   (b) " subtilly like a sheep thought I " (20b).

SHEEP'S EYE, " he cast a sheep's eye at her " (*Epigrams*), ogled, leered : originally to look modestly and with diffidence but always with longing or affection. " That casting a sheepe's eye at hir, away he goes ; and euer since he lies by himselfe and pines away."—Greene, *Francesco's Fortunes* (1590), *Works*, viii. 191.

SHEEP'S FLESH, " he loveth well sheep's flesh that wets his bread in the wool " (70*c*) : Sharman thinks this refers to a broth or jelly made from the sheep's head boiled with the wool ; as also witness the following from a poem attributed to Lydgate—" Of the shepe is cast awaye no thynge ; . . . Of whoos hede boyled, with wull and all, Tere cometh a gely and an oyntement ryal."—*Treatyse of the Horse, the Shepe, and the Goos.*

SHIFT, " shift each one for himself as he can " (90*d*).

SHILLING, " to bring a shilling to ninepence " (66*c*).

SHOE, (*a*) " the shoe will hold with the sole " (67*c*).

(*b*) " now for good luck cast an old shoe after me " (21*d*), an old and still intelligible bit of folk-lore : allusions to it are very numerous in old writers. " Captain, your shoes are old, pray put 'em off, And let one fling 'em after us."—Beaumont and Fletcher, *Honest Man's Fortune* (1613).

(*c*) " myself can tell best where my shoe doth wring me " (69*d*), the moderns substitute " pinch " for " wring." " I wot best, wher wringeth me my sho."—Chaucer, *Cant. Tales* (1383), 9426.

(*d*) " who waiteth for dead men's shoes shall go long barefoot " (45*a*), it is tedious looking forward to inheritances. " You are my maister's sonne, and you looke for his lande ; but they that hope for dead men's shoes may hap go barefoote."—*Two Angry Women of Abington* (1599).

SHOEMAKER'S WIFE, " who is worse shod than the shoemaker's wife " (39*d*), an excuse for lack of something one ought to possess : compare Slipper.

SHOOT, (*a*) " ye shoot nigh the prick " (15*a*), *prick* = point, dot, mark, " bull's-eye."

(*b*) " he shooteth wide " (*Epigrams*).

(*c*) " whom ye see out of the way, or shoot wide, over-shoot not yourself any side to hide " (58*c*).

SHOOTANKER, " her substance is shootanker whereat I shoot " (13*d*), chief support ; *i.e.* the principal attraction as constituting the lady's last chance of marriage.

SHOOTING, " short shooting loseth your game " (97*c*), a technical term in archery : *i.e.* shooting wide of the mark.

SHORE, " ye lean to the wrong shore " (57*b*).

SHORN, " as rich as a new shorn sheep " (42*d*), see Sheep.

SHOT, " pay the shot " (45*d*), *shot*=reckoning, share of expense. " Well at your will ye shall be furnisht. But now a jugling tricke to pay the shot."—Chettle, *Kind Harts Dreame* (1592).

SHREW, " every man can rule a shrew save he that hath her " (75*a*).

SIGHT, " out of sight out of mind " (8*d*), a saying which is found in Thomas à Kempis (1450), and earlier in *Prov. of Hendyng* (*c*. 1320)—" Fer from e3e, fer from herte, Quoth Hendyng."

SIMPER DE COCKET (52*b*), found as a *subs.* as well as an *adj.*=coquettish, wanton. " I saw you dally with your simper de cocket."—Heywood, *Play of Weather* (*Works*, 1. 122*d*). " And gray russet rocket With simper the cocket."—Skelton, *The Tunnyng of Elynoure Rummyng* (1520).

SINK, (*a*) " thou shalt sure sink in thine own sin for us " (28*c*).
    (*b*) " sink or swim " (92*b*).

SIR JOHN (66*d*), generic for a parish priest : our universities . . . confer the designation of Dominus on those who have taken their first degree of Bachelor of Arts ; the word Dominus was naturally translated Sir, and, as almost every clergyman had taken his first degree, it became customary to apply the term to the lower class of the hierarchy.

SIT, " better sit still than rise and fall " (68*c*). " Oh Cousin, I have heard my father say, that it is better to sit fast than to rise and fall, and a great wise man who knew the world to a hayre, would say, that the meane was sure : better be in the middle roome, then either in the Garret or the Sellor."—Brereton, *Court and Country* (1618).

SIX, " set all at six and seven " (38*d*), in confusion, at loggerheads. " Alle in sundur hit [a tun] brast in six or in seuyn."—*Avowyne of King Arther* (*c.* 1340), 64 [Camden Soc., *Eng. Meln. Rom.* 89].

SKIN, (*a*) " a lamb's skin ye will provide . . . to lap her in " (76*c*), see Lamb's skin.

(*b*) " it is good sleeping in a whole skin " (69*a*), this is the title of a play by W. Wager, not now extant.

SKIRTS, " sit on their skirts " (13*b*), pursue, persecute, " go for." " Touching the said archbishop, he had not stood neutrall as was promised, therefore he had justly set on his skirts."—Howell, *Fam. Lett.* (1650).

SKY, " when the sky falleth we shall have larks " (11*c*), a retort to a wild hypothesis; " if pigs had wings they would be likely birds." " Si les nues tomboyent esperoyt prendre les alouettes."—Rabelais, *Gargantua.*

SLANDER, " it may be a slander but it is no lie " (84*c*).

SLEEVE, (*a*) " laughed in my sleeve " (71*a*), derided or exulted in secret.

(*b*) " flattering knaves and flearing queans . . . hang on his sleeve " (66*a*), lickspittle, cadge from, are dependent on.

(*c*) " a broken sleeve holdeth th' arm back " (21*b*). " It is a terme with John and Jacke, Broken sleeve draweth arme a backe."—*Parliament of Byrdes* (1550).

(*d*) " she lacketh but even a new pair of sleeves " (28*a*).

SLEEVELESS ERRAND (17*d*), the origin of " sleeveless " is a matter of conjecture, though its meaning is tolerably clear : thus " a sleeveless (=inadequate) reason " (*Relig, Antiq.*); " a sleeveless (=trifling) excuse " (Lyly); " sleeveless (=aimless) rhymes " (Hall); " a sleeveless (=objectless, wanting cover or excuse, fruitless, fool's) errand " (Chaucer, Shakspeare, &c.). Sharman suggests the mediæval custom of favoured knights wearing the sleeve of their mistress as a mark of favour, aspirants failing to obtain the badge being dubbed " sleeveless "—" Sir Launcelot wore the sleive of the faire maide of Asteloth in a tourney, whereat queene Guenever was much displeased " (Spenser).

SLIPPER, " let not the cobbler wade above his slipper " (*Epigrams*). " Heere are the tenne precepts to be observed in the art of scolding : therefore let not the cobler wade above his slipper. The cobler above his slipper, said Chubb, hee is a knave that made that proverb."—Simon Snel-knave, *Fearefull and Lamentable Effects of Two Dangerous Comets* (1591).

SLIPSTRING, " a waghalter slipstring " (86*d*), a gallows-bird, one rope-ripe but who has cheated the gallows. " Thow art a slipstring I'le warrant."—Lyly, *Mother Bombie* (1594), ii. 1.

SLOTH, " sloth must breed a scab " (9*b*).

SLUGGING, " slugging in bed " (58*a*), lazing. " All night slugging in a cabin."—Spenser, *State of Ireland*.

SMALL, " many small make a great " (37*b*), mod. " many a mickle makes a muckle." " The proverbe saith that many a small makith a grete."—Chaucer, *Parson's Tale* (1383).

SMELLED, " I smelled her out " (39*c*), discovered, " nosed," found. " Can you smell him out by that? " —Shakspeare, *Much Ado* (1600), iii. 2.

SNAIL, " in haste like a snail " (31*d*).

SNEAKBILL, " such a sneakbill " (88*c*), a generic term of contempt. " A checheface, mecher, sneakebill, wretched fellow, one out of whose nose hunger drops." —Cotgrave, *Did.* (1611).

SNOW, " snow is white and lyeth in the dike and every man lets it lie " (62*d*).

SNUDGE, " pinch like a snudge " (83*b*), *snudge* = miser. " Your husbandry . . . is more like the life of a covetous snudge that ofte very evill proves."—Ascham, *Toxoph.* (1544), i.

SOLD, (*a*) " better sold than bought " (27*a*).
     (*b*) " like one to be sold she set out herself in fine apparel " (52*a*).

SOME, " here some and there some " (*Epigrams*).

SOMETHING, " something is better than nothing " (*Epi-grams* and 29*c*, with " somewhat " for " something ").

SOON, " till soon fare ye well " (74*a*), this may=till some future time not far distant, or *soon*=evening, a provincialism.

SORE, " present salve for this present sore " (20*d*).

SORROW, (*a*) " I had sorrow to my sops " (87*d*).
    (*b*) " make not two sorrows of one " (72*d*).
    (*c*) " to bring her solace that bringeth me sorrow " (88*c*).

SOULS, " poor men have no souls " (*Epigrams*).

SOW, (*a*) " as meet as a sow to bear a saddle " (52*c*).
    (*b*) " the still sow eats up all the draff " (27*c*), *still sow*=a generic reproach, a sly lurking fellow ; *draff*=anything unfit for human food. " We do not act, that often jest and laugh ; 'Tis old but true, still swine eat all the draff."—Shakspeare, *Merry Wives of Windsor* (1596), iv. 2.
    (*c*) " grease the fat sow on th' arse (or tail) " (39*a*), be insensible to kindness : see *Scogin's Jests*.
    (*d*) " the sow will no more so deep root " (58*c*).
    (*e*) " (ye took) the wrong sow by the ear " (92*a*), to make a wrong conclusion. " When he has got into one o' your city pounds, the counters, he has the wrong sow by the ear, i' faith ; and claps his dish at the wrong man's door."—Jonson, *Every Man in his Humour* (1596), ii. 7.

SPARE, (*a*) " ever spare and ever bare " (66*c*).
    (*b*) " spare to speak, spare to speed " (38*c*).

SPARK, " this spark of hope have I " (101*a*).

SPEED, " both bade me God speed, but none bade me welcome " (23*c*).

SPIT, " I will spit in my hands and take better hold " (64*c*).

SPOONS, " as nice as it had been a ha'porth of silver spoons " (98*c*).

SPUR, " a gentle white spur and at need a sure spear " (35*a*).

STABLE DOOR, " when the steed is stolen shut the stable door " (26*b*), set a guard after the mischief is done ;

see Barclay, *Ship of Fools* (1509), i. 76 (1874). " Quant le cheval est emblé dounke ferme fols l'estable."— *Les Proverbes del Vilain* (*c.* 1300). " The steede was stollen before I shut the gate, The cates consumed before I smelt the feast."—*Devises of Sundrie Gentlemen.*

STAFF, (*a*) " the worse end of the staff " (58*c*), we now say " wrong end of the stick."
(*b*) " what sendeth he (*i.e.* God), a staff and a wallet? " (66*d*).

STAKE, (*a*) " the loth stake standeth long " (60*d*), see Loath.
(*b*) " it is an ill stake that cannot stand one year in a hedge " (60*d*).
(*c*) " as a bear goeth to the stake " (21*c*).
(*d*) " we shall so part stake, that I shall lose the hole " (67*c*).
(*e*) " hath eaten a stake " (35*b*).

STALE, (*a*) " stale a goose " (42*c*), stole : an old inflection.
(*b*) " stale home to me " (65*b*), see *supra.*

START, " who hopeth in God's help his help cannot start " (11*c*), change, be moved away.

STAVE'S END, " I live here at stave's end " (42*b*).

STAY, " to stay somewhat for her staying " (89*b*), keep back somewhat for a rainy day.

STEINTH, " steinth yet the stoutest " (11*b*), checks, causes to hesitate. " The Reve answered and saide, Stint thy clappe."—Chaucer, *Cant. Tales* (1383), 3144.

STERVETH, " the horse sterveth " (36*d*), starveth : note the rhyme—" serveth "=" sarveth," now vulgar.

STIFF-NECKED (87*c*), untoward, unruly, mulish.

STILE, " ye would be over the stile ere ye come at it " (97*d*). " *Dulipo.* I would fayne have you conclude. *Erostrato.* You would fayne leape over the stile before you come at the hedge."—Gascoigne, *Supposes* (1575).

STOMACH, " an when the meal mouth hath won the bottom of your stomach " (23*d*).

STONE, (a) " the rolling stone never gathereth moss "
(31c), see Moss.
   (b) " I do but roast a stone " (56c), see Roast.

STOOLS, " between two stools my tale go'th to the
ground " (9b), a proverb found in a French manu-
script of the fourteenth century—" Entre deux arcouns
chet cul à terre."—*Les Proverbes del Vilain*, MS.
Bodleian (c. 1300). Afterwards used by Rabelais
(*Gargantua*, liv. i. c. ii.), " S'asseoir entre deux selles
le cul à terre."

STORE, " store is no sore " (12c).

STRAIGHT-LACED (37d), precise, squeamish, puritanical.

STRAINABLE, " sturdy storms strainable " (55a), violent,
strong. " A Portingale ship was driven and drowned
by force of a streinable tempest neere unto the shore
of the Scotish Isles."—Holinshed, *Hist. Scotland:
Josina*.

STRAW, (a) " ye stumbled at a straw and leapt over a
block " (92b), made much of nothing. " Lest of a
strawe we make a block."—*Pilgr. Perf.* [W. de W.,
1531], 93.
   (b) " this gear will breed a pad in the straw "
(*Epigrams*), see Pad.
   (c) " lay a straw here and even there " (63c).
   (d) " thou wilt not step over a straw " (41d), go a
step out of the way.

STREAM, " to strive against the stream " (68b).

STRIFE, " since by strife ye may lose and cannot win,
suffer " (69a).

SUFFERANCE, (a) " sufferance is no quittance " (64d).
   (b) " of sufferance cometh ease " (22b). " Ile give
a proverbe—Sufferance giveth ease."—Marston, *What
you Will* (1607).

SUGAR, (a) " when time hath turned white sugar to
white salt " (6c), otherwise (as 32d), " when sweet
sugar should turn to sour saltpetre."
   (b) " I have for fine sugar fair rat's bane " (80a).

SUMMER, see Swallow.

SUN, " when the sun shineth make hay " (8c), seize
your chance or opportunity.

SURGEON, " I am like the ill surgeon (said I) without store of good plasters " (20*d*).

SWALLOW, " one swallow maketh not summer " (70*a*). " One swallowe prouveth not that summer is neare." —Northbrooke, *Treatise against Dauncing* (1577).

SWEET, (*a*) " sweet meat will have sour sauce " (19*d*).
    (*b*) " take the sweet with the sour " (62*c*).
    (*c*) " sweet sauce began to wax sour " (54*b*).
    (*d*) " sweet beauty with sour beggary " (49*b*).

SWIM, " he must needs swim that is held . up by the chin " (12*d*), see *Scogin's Jests* (1565).

SWORD, (*a*) " he that striketh with the sword shall be stricken with the scabbard " (77*d*), see *Revelation*, xiii. 10. " *Nich.* Blessed be the peace-makers ; they that strike with the sword shall be beaten with the scabbard. *Phil.* Well said, proverbs, nere another to that purpose? *Nich.* Yes, I could have said to you, syr, Take heede is a good reede."—Haughton, *Two Angry Women of Abington* (1599).
    (*b*) " it is ill putting a naked sword in a mad man's hand " (87*c*).

TALE, (*a*) " a tale of a tub " (94*c*), nonsense, fooling, absurdity. " Ye say they follow your law, And vary not a shaw, Which is a tale of a tub."—Bale, *Three Laws* (1538), *Works* (E.E.D.S.).
    (*b*) " a good tale ill told in the telling is marred " (82*c*), see *infra*.
    (*c*) " good tales well told and ill heard . . . are marred " (82*c*), see *supra*.
    (*d*) " to tell tales out of school " (23*d*), to romance, play the informer (Tyndale, *d.* 1536).
    (*e*) " by told tales " (27*c*), *tale*=incredible story, marvellous narration ; also words of wisdom : thus the acme of truth or falsehood. " Telle no talys."—*Cov. Myst.* (1469).

TARIER, " let him be no longer tarier " (35*d*), a dawdler, a " slowcoach." " And for that cause he is often times called of them Fabius cunctator, that is to say, the tarier or delayer."—Elyot, *Governour* (1531), bk. i., ch. xxiii.

TAUNT TIVET (87*d*), primarily a hunting call, a note on the horn : here an exclamatory salutation.

TEETH, " to cast in my teeth checks and choking oysters " (43*c*), see Checks and Choking oysters.

TERMS, " in plain terms plain truth to utter " (54*c*).

THAMES, (*a*) " to cast water in Thames " (39*b*), a simile of useless or thankless labour ; a work of supererogation.
 (*b*) " bearing no more rule than a goose turd in Thames " (76*c*).

THAN (*passim*), then.

THANKLESS, " a thankless office " (58*d*).

THIEF, " to ax my fellow whether I be a thief " (72*b*).

THIEVES, (*a*) " when thieves fall out true men come to their good " (93*b*), or (modern) " when thieves fall out honest men come by their own " : *good*=belongings.
 (*b*) " beggars may sing before thieves and weep before true men " (47*a*).

THING, (*a*) " too much of one thing is not good " (64*d*), this we now shorten to " too much of a good thing."

THOUGHT, (*a*) " thought is free " (57*b*). " Since thought is free, thinke what thou will."—James I., MS. Add. 24,195.
 (*b*) " my thought . . . is a goodly dish " (61*b*).

THREAD, " you spin a fair thread " (68*c*), with which compare " this thread finer to spin " (12*d*).

THREE, (*a*) " three may keep counsel if two be away " (165*b*). " Three may keep a counsel if twain be away."—Chaucer, *Ten Commandments of Love.* " The empress, the midwife, and yourself : Two may keep counsel, when the third's away."—Shakspeare, *Titus Andronicus* (1593), iv. 2.
 (*b*) " frenzy, heresy, and jealousy are three that . . . never cured be " (77*c*).

THRIFT, (*a*) " when thrift is in the town ye be in the field " (92*a*).
 (*b*) " I will now begin thrift when thrift seemeth gone " (93*d*).

(c) " now thrift is gone now would ye thrive in all haste " (95b).

(d) " thou art past thrift before thrift begin " (35a).

(e) " when thrift and you fell first at a fray you played the man, for ye made thrift run away " (42d).

THRIVE, " he that will thrive must ask leave of his wife " (34d), another form of which occurs in Thynn's *Deb. betw. Pride and Lowliness* (1570) :—" He had a sonne or twaine he would advaunce, And sayd they should take paines untyll it fell ; He that wyll thrive (quod he) must tary chaunce."

THUMB, (a) " ye taunt me tit over thumb " (64a).

(b) " she hitteth me on the thumbs " (64a).

(c) " this biteth the mare by the thumb " (76c).

TICKING, " then ticking might have taught any young couple their love ticks to have wrought " (53d)— " leave lewd ticking " (70d)—" to tick and laugh with me he hath lawful leave " (71a), tick = to dally, wanton : frequently " tick and toy." " Such ticking, such toying, such smiling, such winking, and such manning them home when the sports are ended."—Gosson, *School of Abuse* (1579).

TICKLE, " my tongue must oft tickle " (15b), itch to be wagging (Udall, *Apoph.* 381).

TIDE, " the tide tarrieth no man " (8c). " Hoist up saile while gale doth last, Tide and wind stay no man's pleasure."—Southwell, *St. Peter's Complaint* (1595).

TIME, (a) " take time when time cometh, lest time steal away " (8c).

(b) " let time try " (72c).

(c) " time trieth truth " (72c).

(d) " time is tickle " (8d), uncertain.

(e) " time lost again we cannot win " (51d).

TIPPETS, " so turned they their tippets " (54c), changed right about : cf. " turncoat "; frequently of girls on marriage. " Another Bridget ; one that for a face Would put down Vesta ; You to turn tippet ! "— Jonson, *Case is Altered* (1609).

TIT, (a) " tit for tat " (64a), blow for blow, an equivalent, as good one side as the other : *i.e.* Fr., *tant
pour tant*.
   (b) " little tit, all tail " (24c), *tit* originally=any-
thing very small or diminutive.

TITIFILS, " no more such titifils " (24a), a knave, a
jade : a generic reproach. " The devill hymself . . .
did apparell certain catchepoules and parasites, commonly called titivils and tale tellers, to sowe discord
and dissencion."—Hall, *Henry VI.* (1542), f. 43.

TOAD, " she swelled like a toad " (39b).

TOAST, " hot as a toast " (54b).

TONE (*passim*), the one : see Tother.

TONGUE, (a) " her tongue runneth on pattens " (78a),
see Pattens.
   (b) " let not your tongue run at rover " (69a), see
Rover.
   (c) " thy tongue runneth before thy wit " (64a).
   (d) " biteth not with teeth but with her tongue "
(75b).
   (e) " her tongue is no edged tool but yet it will cut "
(24b).
   (f) " tongue breaketh bone, itself having none "
(68c). " Tonge breketh bon, Ant nad hire selve non."
—*Proverbs of Hendyng*, MS. (c. 1320).
   (g) " when your tongue tickleth, at will let it walk "
(15d).
   (h) " my tongue must oft tickle " (15b), itch to be
wagging.
   (i) " it hurteth not the tongue to give fair words "
(22b). " O, madam, faire words never hurt the
tongue."—Jonson, &c., *Eastward Hoe* (1605).
   (j) " he may show wisdom at will that with angry
heart can hold his tongue still " (44d).
   (k) " I would thy tongue were cooled to make thy
tales more cold " (85c).
   (l) " my tongue is a limb to match and to vex
every vein of him " (68b).
   (m) " think ye . . . I will be tongued-tied " (69c).

TOOTING, " on my maids he is ever tooting " (70*b*), making signals to.

TOP, " as soon drive a top over a tiled house " (71*c*).

TOTHER (*passim*), the other : see Tone.

TOTT'N'AM, " Tott'n'am was turned French " (17*d*), said of great alterations and changed conditions : from the migration of a number of French workmen to this locality early in the reign of Henry VIII., their competition provoking the jealousy of English mechanics, and resulting in disturbances in the streets of London on May-day, 1517.

TOW, " more tow on their distaves than they can well spin " (73*c*), more in hand than can be well undertaken. " I have more tow on my dystaffe than I can well spyn."—Heywood, *Works* (E.E.D.S.), 1. 25*c*.

TOY, (*a*) " every trifling toy age cannot laugh at " (88*a*), *toy* = whim, fancy, jest, &c.
   (*b*) " such toys in her head " (75*b*), see *supra*.
   (*c*) " their faces told toys " (17*d*), see Face.

TRACT, " tract of time " (8*a*), process, length, continued duration. " This in tracte of tyme made hym welthy." Fabyan, *Chronycle*, ch. lvi.

TRADE, " yourself taketh direct trade " (14*c*), way, means, course. " The Jewes, emong whom alone and no moe, God hitherto semed for to reigne, by reason of their knowledge of the law, and of the autoritee of being in the right trade of religion."—Udall, *Luke* xix.

TREASON, " in trust is treason " (67*c*).

TREE, (*a*) " it were a folly for me to put my hand between the bark and the tree " (57*d*), to meddle in family matters.
   (*b*) " timely crooketh the tree that would a cammock be " (94*a*), see Cammock.
   (*c*) " you cannot see the wood for trees " (62*b*), see Wood.

TRIP, " take me in any trip " (59*d*).

TRUE, " it must needs be true that every man sayeth " (38*a*).

TRUTH, (*a*) " tell truth without sin " (28*a*).

(*b*) " deem the best till time hath tried the truth out " (72*d*), see Time.

TUN, " as full as a tun " (45*b*), *tun* = a large cask. " And ever sith hath so the tappe yronne, Til that almost all empty is the tonne."—Chaucer, *Cant. Tales* (1383), 3,891.

TUNE, (*a*) " out of tune by note " (68*c*).

(*b*) " no tale could tune you in time to take heed " (90*c*).

TURD, (*a*) " one crop of a turd marreth a pot of potage " (76*d*).

(*b*) " the more we stir a turd, the more it will stink " (76*d*).

TURN, " one good turn asketh another " (41*c*) : we now say " deserves."

TWAIN, " we twain are one too many " (65*b*).

UNBORN, " better unborn than untaught " (25*a*). " Old men yn proverbe sayde by old tyme, ' A chyld were beter to be unbore, Than to be untaught."—Symon, *Lessons of Wysedome for all Maner Chyldryn* (*c.* 1450).

UNKISSED, (*a*) " farewell, unkissed " (29*d*), of a not over-friendly parting : see next entry.

(*b*) " unknown, unkissed " (38*c*).

UNMINDED, " unminded, unmoaned " (21*c*).

URE (*passim*), chance, destiny, fortune, use, practice.

USE, " use maketh maistry " (55*d*), *maistry* = mastery, perfection.

VENOM, " spit her venom " (24*d*).

VIAGE, " this viage make " (21*c*), *voyage* = a journey by land or sea. " To Scotland now he fondes, to redy his viage."—*Robert de Brunne*, 314.

f

WADE, " for what should I further wade " (43*a*).

WAGHALTER, " waghalter slipstring " (86*d*), *waghalter*
=a rogue, gallowsbird, crackrope: see Slipstring.
" I'll teach my wag-halter to know grapes from
barley."—Lyly, *Mother Bombie* (1594), ii. 5.

WALK, (*a*) " walk, drab, walk ! " (63*c*).
   (*b*) " walk, knave, walk ! " (63*c*).

WALKING-STAFF, " the walking-staff hath caught warmth
in your hand " (26*c*).

WALL, (*a*) " to winch or kick against the hard wall "
(68*b*), *winch* (or *wince*)=kick. " Paul, whom the
Lord hadde chosun, long tyme wynside agen the
pricke."—Wycliffe, *Prolog on the Dedes of Apostles.*
   (*b*) " further than the wall he cannot go " (71*b*).
   (*c*) " drive him to the wall " (71*b*), urge to extremities, " corner."
   (*d*) " I shall pike out no more than out of the stone
wall " (72*b*), *pike*=pick, find out, learn, mark.
   (*e*) " as in frost a mud wall cracketh and crumbleth
so melteth his money " (79*a*).

WALTHAM, " as wise as Waltham's calf " (58*d*), the
allusion is lost though the meaning is clear and
examples are many, the earliest I have found occurring in Skelton's *Colin Clout* (1520), where a rascal
priest is described " As wyse as Waltom's calfe . . .
he can nothyng smatter Of logyke nor scole matter."
" Some running and gadding calves, wiser than
Waltham's calfe that ranne nine miles to sucke a
bull."—*Disclosing of the great Bull* [*Harl. Misc.*
(1567), vii. 535].

WAN, " I wan them " (42*a*), won.

WARS, " we do much wars " (39*a*), worse : note the
rhyme.

WASH, " as sober as she seemeth, five days come about
but she will once wash her face in an ale clout "
(26*d*).

WASP, " angry as a wasp " (31*b*).

WATER, (a) " the trial thereof we will lay a water "
(10a)—" my matter is laid a water " (*Epigrams*), see
Lay.
  (b) " you come to look in my water " (41a), physi-
cians once diagnosed complaints by " casting the
water of a patient." " If thou could'st, doctor, cast
The water of my land, find her disease."—Shakspeare,
Macbeth (1606), v. 3.
  (c) " there was no more water than the ship drew "
(89a).

WATER-DRINKER, " a falser water-drinker there liveth
not " (72a).

WAX, " at my will I weened she should have wrought
like wax " (75a).

WAY, " if ye haul this way I will another way draw "
(63d).

WEAKER, " the weaker hath the worse " (23b).

WEALTH, (a) " both for wealth and woe " (17a), *wealth*
=(originally) good, weal, prosperity. " Let no man
seek his own, but every man another's wealth."—
I *Corinth.* (*Auth. Ver.*, 1611), x. 24.
  (b) " all thing may be suffered saving wealth "
(62b).

WEATHER, (a) " when all shrews have dined, change from
foul weather to fair is oft inclined " (50c).
  (b) " weather meet to set paddocks abroad in "
(50b), see Paddocks.

WEATHERCOCK, " like a weathercock " (102a).

WED, " where nought is to wed with wise men flee the
clog " (32a).

WEDDED, " I was wedded unto my will . . . I will be
divorced and be wed to my wit " (102c).

WEDDETH, " who weddeth ere he be wise shall die ere
he thrive " (19b).

WEDDING (TERMS OF), (a) " wooing for woeing, banna
for banning, the banns for my bane, marrying marring,
a woman, as who saith, woe to the man " (83c).

(b) " wedding and hanging are destiny " (9c), an earlier mention, " Hanging and wiving go by destiny," is found in the *Schole-hous for Women* (1541). In 1558 a ballad was licensed with the title " The Proverbe is true y⁺ Weddynge in destinyē."

(c) " they went (witless) to wedding whereby at last they both went a-begging " (33d).

(d) " quick wedding may bring good speed " (10a).

WEED, (a) " ill weeds groweth fast " (27d). " Ewyl weed ys sone y-growe."—*MS. Harleian* (c. 1490).

(b) " the weed overgroweth the corn " (27d).

WEEK, " in by the week " (84b).

WEEP, " better children weep than old men " (*Epigrams*), see Man.

WELCOME, " welcome when thou goest " (79d).

WELL, (a) " all is well that ends well " (25c).

(b) " believe well and have well " (90d).

(c) " do well and have well " (90d).

WET FINGER, " with a wet finger " (95c), easily, readily : as easy as turning over the leaf of a book, rubbing out writing on a slate, or tracing a lady's name on the table with spilt wine—the last may well be the origin of the phrase : cf. " Verba leges digitis, verba notata mero " (Ovid, *Amor.* i. 4. 20). So also Tibullus, lib. i. el. 6 :—" Neu te decipiat nutu, digitoque liquorem Ne trahat, et mensæ ducat in orbe notas." " What gentlewomen or citizens' wives you can with a wet finger have at any time to sup with you."— Dekker, *The Gull's Hornbook* (1602).

(d) " many wells, many buckets " (85b).

WHELP, " as a whelp for wantonness in and out whips " (17c).

WHIT, " as good never a whit as never the better " (102b).

WHITE LIVERED (69c), cowardly, mean : an old notion was that cowards had bloodless livers. " White liver'd runagate."—Shakspeare, *Richard III.* (1597), iv. 1.

WHITENESS, " that all her whiteness lieth in her white hairs " (4c), *whiteness*=chastity.

WHITING, " there leaped a whiting " (78d), there was an opportunity missed.

WHOLE, (a) " if ye lack that away ye must wind with your whole errand and half th' answer behind " (51c).
(b) " hear the whole, the whole wholly to try " (50a).

WHORE, " hop whore pipe thief " (86d).

WIFE, (a) " he that will thrive must ask leave of his wife " (34d) : a variant is " it is hard to wive and thrive both in a year " (34d). " A man may not wyfe And also thryfe And alle in a yere."—*Towneley Mysteries* (c. 1420).
(b) " the best or worst thing to man for this life is good or ill choosing his good or ill wife " (6b).
(c) " a good wife maketh a good husband " (88c).

WILL, (a) " he that will not when he may, when he would, he shall have nay " (8a), with which compare " who that may not as they would, will as they may " (68a).
(b) " when we would, ye would not . . . wherefore now when ye would, now will not we " (28b).
(c) " that one will not, another will " (8d).
(d) " will will have will, though will woe win " (35a).
(e) " will is a good son and will is a shrewd boy and wilful shrewd will hath wrought thee this toy " (35a).

WILLING, " nothing is impossible to a willing heart " (11c).

WIN, (a) " will may win my heart " (11d).
(b) " although I nought win yet shall I nought lose " (102a).
(c) " ye can nought win by any wayward mean " (68d).
(d) " he playeth best that wins " (*Epigrams*).

WINCH, see Wall (*a*).

WIND, (*a*) " an ill wind that bloweth no man to good "
(93*c*). " *Falstaff.* What wind blew you hither, Pistol?
Pistol. Not the ill wind which blows no man to good."
—Shakspeare, *2 Henry IV.* (1598), v. 3.
(*b*) " let this wind overblow " (36*c*).
(*c*) " every wind bloweth not down the corn "
(93*d*).
(*d*) " all this wind shakes no corn " (36*c*).
. (*e*) " I smelt her out and had her straight in the
wind " (39*c*), had at an advantage ; understood her.
(*f*) " I have him in the wind " (*Epigrams*), see
supra.
(*g*) " what wind bloweth ye hither? " (25*a*).
(*h*) " to take wind and tide with me " (36*c*).
(*i*) " if the wind stand in that door, it standeth
awry " (68*c*). " It is even so? is the winde in that
doore? "—Gascoigne, *Supposes* (1566).
(*j*) " your meddling . . . may bring the wind calm
between us " (59*d*).
(*k*) " I will . . . ill winds to sway, spend some
wind . . . though I waste wind in vain " (60*a*), *wind*
=breath is ancient. " Woman thy wordis and thy
wynde thou not waste."—*York Plays* (*c.* 1362), 258.
(*l*) " knew which way the wind blew " (91*b*), aware
of the position of matters, state of affairs.
(*m*) " wavering as the wind " (54*d*).

WINDFALL, " to win some windfall " (38*d*).

WINE, " ye praise the wine before ye taste of the grape "
(27*d*).

WING, " keep your bill under wing mute " (69*a*).

WISE, (*a*) " ye are wise enough if ye keep ye warm "
(56*c*).
(*b*) " better to be happy than wise " (75*c*).
(*c*) " as ye can seem wise in words be wise in
deed " (73*b*).
(*d*) " every wise man staggers in earnest or boord
to be busy or bold with his biggers or betters " (47*d*).

WISHERS, " wishers and woulders be no good house-
holders " (32*b*). " Wysshers and wolders ben smal

housholders."—*Vulg. Stambrigi* (1510). "He . . . resolved rather to live by his wit, then any way to be pinched with want, thinking this old sentence to be true, the wishers and woulders were never good house-holders."—Green, *Never too Late* (1590).

Wist, "beware of Had I wist" (6c), an exclamation of regret. "Be welle war of wedyng, and thynk in youre thought 'Had I wist' is a thyng it servys of nought."—*Towneley Myst.* (c. 1420).

Wit, (a) "wit is never good till it be bought" (18d), *wit* = wisdom, knowledge. "Stationers could not live, if men did not beleeve the old saying, that Wit bought is better then Wit taught."—*Conceits, Clinches, Flashes and Whimzies* (1639).
(b) "to leave my wit before it leave me" (55c).
(c) "at our wit's end" (18d).
(d) "one good forewit is worth two afterwits" (19a).

Woe, "she hath wrought her own woe" (25d).

Wolf, (a) "to keep the wolf from the door" (83b).
(b) "a wolf in a lamb's skin" (28a).

Wonder, "this wonder lasted nine days" (53b). "Eke wonder last but nine deies never in town."—Chaucer, *Troilus and Creseide.* "A book on any subject by a peasant, or a peer, is no longer so much as a nine-days wonder."—Ascham, *Schoole-master* (1570).

Wondered, "he that doth as most men do, shall be least wondered on" (56a).

Wood, (a) "there be more ways to the wood than one" (93d).
(b) "thou art so wood" (86c)—"she was horn wood" (99c), mad, furious, frantic, raging. "Flemynges, lyke wood tygres."—Fabyan, *Cronycle* (an. 1299).
(c) "ye cannot see the wood for trees" (62b). "From him who sees no wood for trees And yet is busie as the bees . . . Libera nos."—*A Letany for S. Omers* (1682).
(d) "ye took the wrong way to the wood" (92a).

WOOL, (a) " what should your face thus again the wool be shorn? " (36c).

(b) " thy face is shorn against the wool, very deep " (*Epigrams*).

(c) " bolster or pillow for me, be whose woll—I will not bear the devil's sack " (73d).

WORD, (a) " not afford you one good word " (93b).

(b) " one ill word axeth another " (22a).

(c) " many words, many buffets " (85b).

(d) " good words bring not ever of good deeds good hope " (94a).

(e) " this doth sound . . . on your side in words, but on my side in deeds " (83d).

(f) " few words to the wise suffice " (82c).

WORKMAN, " what is a workman without his tools? " (94c).

WORLD, (a) " the world runneth on wheels " (78b), runs easily, expeditiously.

(b) " let the world wag " (12d), let go, let things take care of themselves. " Y'are a baggage ; the Slies are no rogues ; Look in the chronicles, we came in with Richard Conqueror. Therefore, paucas pallabris ; let the world slide."—Shakspeare, *Taming of the Shrew*. Induction i. 6.

(c) " he brought the world so about " (98d).

WORM, " tread a worm on the tail and it must turn again " (64c). " The smallest worm will turn, being trodden on ; And doves will peck in safe-guard of their brood."—Shakspeare, 3 *Henry VI*. (1595), ii. 2.

WORSE, " all thing is the worse for the wearing " (54a).

WORST, (a) " provide for the worst, while the best itself save " (12d).

(b) " the worst is behind, we come not where it grew " (57c).

(c) " if the worst fell, we could have but a nay " (44c).

WOT, " I wot what I wot " (84d).

WRONG, " thou beggest at wrong door " (*Epigrams*)—
" ye beg at a wrong man's door " (20*c*).

YEAR, " I am too old a year " (90*c*).

YESTERDAY, (*a*) " it is too late to call again yesterday "
(90*b*).
(*b*) " the offence of yesterday I may redeem " (90*b*).

YIELD, " in case as ye shall yield me as ye cast me, so
shall ye cast me as ye yield me " (43*c*).

YOUNG, " ye be young enough to mend, but I am too
old to see it " (90*c*).

YOUNGER, " ye shall never labour younger " (21*c*), see
Labour.

YOW (*passim*), you.

R. CLAY AND SONS, LTD., BREAD ST. HILL, E.C., AND BUNGAY, SUFFOLK.